Flying on His Wings

*Living Above Daily Struggles:
Taking Flight with God*

Lisa Buffaloe

Flying on His Wings

© 2015 Lisa Buffaloe (updated 070523).
Visit the author at: https://lisabuffaloe.com
Published by John 15:11 Publications

All rights reserved. No part of this book may be reproduced or transmitted in any way, form or by any means, electronic or mechanical—including photocopying, recording, or by any information storage and retrieval system— except brief quotations in printed reviews – without permission of the author.

Cover design by Scott Buffaloe

ISBN: 978-0692336724
ASIN: B016IPRMX8

Scripture taken from the New Century Version® (NCV). Copyright © 2005 by Thomas Nelson, Inc. Used by permission. All rights reserved.

Living Bible (TLB) The Living Bible copyright © 1971 by Tyndale House Foundation. Used by permission of Tyndale House Publishers Inc., Carol Stream, Illinois 60188. All rights reserved.

Scripture taken from the NEW AMERICAN STANDARD BIBLE® (NASB), Copyright © 1960, 1962, 1963 ,1968, 1971, 1972, 1973 ,1975, 1977, 1995 by The Lockman Foundation. Used by permission.

Scripture quotations marked (NLT) are taken from the Holy Bible, New Living Translation, copyright © 1996, 2004, 2007 by Tyndale House Foundation. Used by permission of Tyndale House Publishers, Inc., Carol Stream, Illinois 60188. All rights reserved.

THE HOLY BIBLE, NEW INTERNATIONAL VERSION®, NIV® Copyright © 1973, 1978, 1984, 2011 by Biblica, Inc.™ Used by permission. All rights reserved worldwide.

Scripture taken from the New King James Version®. Copyright © 1982 by Thomas Nelson, Inc. Used by permission. All rights reserved.

Scripture taken from *The Message*. Copyright © 1993, 1994, 1995, 1996, 2000, 2001, 2002. Used by permission of NavPress Publishing Group.

Scripture quotations marked HCSB are taken from the Holman Christian Standard Bible®, Copyright © 1999, 2000, 2002, 2003, 2009 by Holman Bible Publishers. Used by permission. Holman Christian Standard Bible®, Holman CSB®, and HCSB® are federally registered trademarks of Holman Bible Publishers. Scripture marked ERV, Copyright ©2006 World Bible Translation Center.

Flying on His Wings

Contents

Buckle Your Seatbelt 1

Baggage Handling 42

Trusting The Pilot 75

Flying Through the Battle While Battling Through the Flight 98

Catching Air Currents 124

Flying Forward 158

Dedication and Thanks 166

About The Author 167

Books by Lisa Buffaloe 168

Notes and Bibliography 171

Buckle Your Seatbelt

Wouldn't it be cool to fly, to have wings, and ride the air currents? Personally I would prefer flying where the air is the perfect temperature, the skies have the best view, and I never get hurt.

Years ago, broken, split-open, and crying, I sat in a chair during late-night worship at a writer's conference. For years God had gently wooed me to allow Him to heal my past, trust Him, and follow where He would lead.

As I submitted to God's gentle process, He brought healing, and then beckoned transparency to share with others how He truly can heal the wounds of our past.

(Okay I'll be honest, the gentle process was from God, but I didn't make it easy. I whined, ran the other way, curled up and cried like a baby, ignored Him, fought Him, and basically kicked and screamed through

God's gentle process. I'm the one who made that process anything but gentle. My stubborn, scared self wasn't sure what to think, but God won, and I'm so glad He won.)

Back to the story... Being transparent is a scary thing. I didn't want to face my past much less tell anyone what had happened. When I finally said "yes" and surrendered, the whisper in my soul responded, "***Buckle your seatbelt ... get ready to fly.***"

I was excited thinking my flight path would include sprouting wings with effortless flying. A cape would be nice with some super-cool outfit to fight crime and the injustices of life. I was ready to fly!

Unfortunately, I had overlooked what else God shared – "***Buckle your seatbelt.***"

Uh oh.

"Buckle your seatbelt" doesn't only indicate takeoff; it also may mean rough weather ahead, storms are coming, the flight is going to be bumpy.

"Buckle your seatbelt" means you better be strapped into your seat because it's going to be a wild ride and you may need a barf bag.

Bummer.

My flight path had already resulted in

scars, bumps, and bruises. I preferred to fly on God's wings—fly high, way high, **super-high** above the past and into the future.

I'll share why I thought flying a few thousand feet above the problems of this world sounded like a good idea. Even though I was raised in a Christian home by parents who loved the Lord, loved one another, and loved their children, many difficulties were going on behind the scenes. No one knew, including my family, what was happening.

At the age of four I was molested by a baby-sitter. As a teenager I was attacked by two guys. I've been chased by a man with a knife. I've also had a shotgun pointed at me as two men tried to run my car off the road. I've been drugged and locked up. I've been stalked and divorced. I've been raped.

As of this writing, I've had numerous surgeries along with numerous medical procedures, biopsies, and hospitalizations. I've had cancer, chronic illness for almost twelve years, moved over thirty times, and experienced many other really nasty things.

Most of my life I flapped my little Buffaloe wings in an attempt to manage life on my own. Although I had dealt with some stuff, I didn't deal with any of the major stuff. I stuffed that stuff.

As a young girl, I didn't understand what happened, and Satan is good at heaping shame on victims to keep them silenced, so I locked the memories away in a closet of my mind.

I told myself if something bad happened again, I couldn't survive. When I was attacked again, I didn't want to live. However, I didn't want to disappoint my parents, so instead of killing myself, I killed off that part of my past. Each experience was stuffed and locked in its own closet because I sure didn't want to open up a previous closet.

Needless to say, I had tons of closets.

During my childhood I had read in Isaiah 43:18 we are told to "forget the former things" and not dwell on the past. That verse sounded good and was easier than having to deal with reality. However, stuffing stuff results in stuff unstuffing, and my stuffing leaked out in various unsightly ways.

How we process (or don't process) can impact our life to hinder or propel. Each of us deals with our difficulties in various methods -- some good, some not so good, and some downright bad. The past leaks out of us in the way we react to others, to ourselves, and to God.

My memory stuffing may not have been the best way to process, but it did give me the ability to not focus on the negative. I can honestly say I've had a great life, just with some really hard times. I didn't note the dates or build memorials of the bad things, and for that I'm grateful.

I've always appreciated another verse in Isaiah which reads, "When you pass through the waters, I will be with you. When you cross rivers, you will not drown. When you walk through fire, you will not be burned, nor will the flames hurt you" (Isaiah 43:2, NCV).

The verse doesn't say we won't go through the deep waters or encounter fiery trials, but that God promises to be with us as we go through whatever we go through.

Looking back, I can see God's lifelines. When I was a young girl in elementary school, my family moved again to another city. On the school bus the other kids wouldn't allow me to sit down unless the bus driver forced them (call me Forestina Gump). School was hard, and the teacher was mean. I was lonely, and I really didn't want to live.

Then in the mail a letter came from a

teenager who had been my sweet babysitter when I was younger. My friend encouraged me and told me I was loved and wanted. I held on to that lifeline. Decades later, I still have that letter.

God's lifelines may not be big and may not even be noticeable at the time, but through the hardship and pain, God's tender touch is always there to help. God's touch may come through the hug of a friend, the smile of a stranger, or through the beauty of His creation.

How many times have you talked to someone who said, "*I wouldn't have made it through if it hadn't been for...*" and they list a person, some kind of provision, or something they saw or experienced. Something helped them make it through, and that "thing" wasn't just luck.

James 1:17 tells us every good thing and every perfect gift is from above.[1] Those good things came from God. It's not just "luck" you've made it through your life. If you're reading this book, you're a survivor. You're still here, still breathing, and still overcoming (High-five and fist-bump!).

Even if you can't see your lifeline, whether you've seen God's hand or not, He has helped you through whatever you've been through, and He will be with you whatever comes next.

God knows the plans He has for you, plans for your welfare and not for calamity to give you a future and a hope.[2] And that hope is a lifeline, a rope, to God's love and goodness.

People may say there are things you will never get over. However, what's interesting about that statement is whatever you are trying to get over, you've already gone through.

We don't have to get over any "thing", because no "thing" is impossible for God. That means every "thing" is possible for God to restore, redeem, heal, and renew.

When Jesus offers forgiveness for those who believe in His name and truly repent of their sins, they are forgiven. When Jesus says He came to heal the brokenhearted and bind their wounds, He didn't just mean a partial healing, but complete soul-healing. We either believe God or we don't.

The memories of my past situations weren't erased, yet I know God has healed them (and continues to heal them). I know my Redeemer lives, and I live in my Redeemer. I know that everything I've been through God has equipped me to not only have gone through and survive, but to also live in a daily new life with Him.

God's mercies are new every morning. His mercies are there when a negative memory resurfaces. His mercies tenderly heal internal and external wounds. His mercies turn around whatever the enemy meant for evil and turns it into good.

Whatever you've gone through, you survived. You are a survivor! You are a gladiator who has been in the ring with the lions and tigers, and you survived. There may be scars, there may be negative memories, there may be heartache and pain, but you survived.

You are a warrior who survived the battle, and because you survived, you are here to point others to The One who helps us through every battle.

The Bible shows life wasn't easy for those who followed God. Most of the journeys were filled with hardships. Jesus' disciples were beaten, stoned, beheaded, thrown in prisons, crucified, killed or exiled. And the early church was persecuted in horrific ways.

And yet, and yet, **and yet**... they wrote of the joy of the Lord. They wrote of the absolute, amazing joy and blessings encountered with a life in Christ. And even during their horrible sufferings, their faith changed the world.

We are also given opportunities to change the world. One life touched in the name of Jesus will be a life changed, and that one life will touch other lives. The ripple effect of our actions and prayers can change lives throughout the world.

As we overcome, as we look back to see God's lifelines, we too can leave lifelines and be part of God's divine rescue. Whatever God has helped you through, show others the faithfulness of God and be part of the rescue lifelines.

Stories worth reading are never boring. There's something amazing about those who survived devastating loss, or went through incredible hardships, or have had wild adventures.

Your story matters. What you've gone through, what you've learned, how God has healed and helped you is an amazing story. No matter who you are, you've gone through something that can help someone else.

Each of us can find life in the hardships, the trials, and the suffering and then share the lifeline of Christ with others.

The Israelites were in Egypt over 400 years and spent much of that time in captivity. The Bible doesn't share much about the captive years, but sure does tell us about God's amazing rescue.

I wonder sometimes if we spend so much time processing our time in captivity we fail to see God's rescue. His deliverance is often missed or dismissed because the focus is on the timing or how we thought the rescue would come. And then all the ways God worked (and is working) was, or is, completely missed.

Now personally I prefer a rescue before a bad thing happens -- like the damsel in distress who is rescued by the knight in shining armor. Uh, but then I remember the damsel <u>was in distress</u>.

Bummer. I guess rescues don't take place unless one is needed.

I suppose the only way to get out of the negatives of life, is not to have a life. And not having a life sounds kind of negative. And since you're reading this book, that means you are breathing and living. And well, that means there are going to be difficulties.

Fortunately, God promises to get us through, and not just through, but safely home with Him.

God's rescues take place with the back against the Red Sea, in the Lion's den, and in the fiery furnace. And oh how they take place in the quiet moments of grief, in the desperate moments of pain, and in the tender moments of healing.

Rescue will come. God's rescue will always come.

Jesus said He came to set the captives free, and when He sets us free, we will indeed be free.[3] Freedom in Christ is freedom from sin (talk about a wonderful rescue!), freedom with new life, and freedom for eternity.

I have a choice when I look at my past to say I was rescued by God or deserted by God. Bad things did happen. Mean people did mean things. I went through nasty situations. The key is God helped me through, and not a moment of that pain has been wasted.

Whether I faced my past or stuffed the memories, every difficulty made alterations in my soul. Yet nothing I've been through hindered God's perfect plan.

Nothing in the past or what will be faced in the future is too big for God. And nothing (except us) can hinder what God wants to do in us and for us.

There is an amazing and wonderful "and yet..." with God. Satan is real and is out to steal, kill, and destroy, **and yet** God is there to restore, bring new life, and redeem. There are many "and yet" moments in each of our lives, and the "and yet" realities, last eternally.

All my difficulties have been replaced with "and yet" God did something amazing from the pain. I'm not alone. The Bible doesn't gloss over the failures and suffering of people, and yet God made somebody out of nobodies, restored what had been taken by enemies, and gave new life and new hope.

To top off the good news, even if there are heartaches and pain, the happy-ever-after comes to those who follow Christ. (Man, we get the best trip ever. And we don't even have to pack or pay for movers, or even unpack! Custom-made home for eternity by the One who made eternity! Woot!)

I'm very grateful when I can look back and see how God worked. After certain difficulties, the world says you'll never be the same, yet God's healing and restoring is available for everyone. Just as a broken bone after mending is actually stronger, those broken places in lives healed by God are only made stronger and the testimony more powerful.

I love how the Bible shows how God worked in the lives of people throughout generations, and I'm grateful for the testimonies of friends who have been through trials and share about God's help and provision.

The 20/20 backward look is great, but the day-to-day is shrouded in mystery and the unknown. The "and yet" isn't yet, so the challenge is to live in the present. In the journey of life, we don't always get a window seat. We can't see beyond the moment.

My body does not travel well. I've been car-sick, sea-sick, air-sick, and land-sick. Movement makes me nauseous. If I'm on a boat (oh, please don't put me on a boat), I have to keep my eyes focused on the horizon. If I'm in a car, I must keep looking forward. When flying on an airplane, if I don't look outside and ground myself, my stomach gets queasy, and my little brain gets all discombobulated. A window seat is most important for the sake of myself and my fellow passengers. Plus, I want to see the journey and know where I'm going.

We can't see with human eyes what's coming next, but God is already there to meet every need. God knows the future, and He never leaves or forsakes us.

In Matthew chapter six, Jesus tells us to not worry about tomorrow because our loving God knows our every need. Therefore, even when life makes us queasy and uneasy, God's mighty hand will never let us go.

I'll admit I do wish I could see the future. Okay let me change that thought ... I'd like to see the future with all the happy stuff. Hmmm. Maybe that's why we don't see the future here on earth. I'm grateful God lets us know in the end, for those who love Him and follow Him, the future will be amazingly awesome.

Have you ever watched a suspenseful movie without knowing the ending? The intensity can keep you on the edge of your seat wondering if the hero or heroine will survive and have a happily-ever-after. However, during a second showing, you can sit confidently because you know the ending.

God knows the ending, knows every moment of our lives, and is here now to walk with us, and is already in the future to be with us during every step. God wants us to live fully in each moment, truly living in the freedom of Christ.

So how do we live in that freedom? I explored that topic as I prepared for a weekend-long retreat where I would be speaking on "Living Joyfully Free." The information came easily at first. Goodness, I've blogged and written books and had plenty of material, but I got stuck as I pondered "living" and "life."

So I read and researched, dug in the Bible, and yet the heavens seemed silent. I shut myself in my office, prayed more, read more, studied more, and begged God for help.

Truthfully I was miserable and void of answers, so I shut myself off from the world. And several weeks later it occurred to me that in the sequestering of myself I had forgotten to actually live the life God had given me.

Seriously? Living life is living life? Could it be that easy?

The Bible tells us Jesus didn't just offer a fire insurance policy to get out of hell. Jesus came to give us life – eternal, unfailing life in abundance – a life filled with His joy and His peace, here and now (day by day and moment by moment). Jesus said Satan came to steal, kill, and destroy, but Jesus came to give us life in abundance.[4]

The definition of abundantly is **superadded, supremely, something further, more, much more than all, superior, extraordinary**, uncommon, more eminent, more remarkable, **more excellent**....

The original Greek gives additional insights. (No need to be a Bible scholar, blueletterbible.org and other websites gives the capacity to type in a verse and find the definitions.) The Greek word for life is ***zō-á*** which means vitality, animate, the absolute fullness of life, real and genuine, active, vigorous, and blessed. And the definition of "living" and "live" is ***zaō*** – to live, breathe, to enjoy real life, to have true life, active, blessed, endless in the kingdom of God, living water, having vital power in itself and exerting the same upon the soul, to be in full vigor, to be fresh, strong, efficient, active, powerful, efficacious, lively, quick.

Oh my goodness, I want a vigorous, strong, blessed, superadded, superior extraordinary life! Talk about flying! Yes, please. May I have that kind of life the rest of my days? Please, God? May I, please?

I wish I could tell you as a long-term Christian I've got this Christian life down to a science, I have life all together, and never have bad days. But to be honest, there are days my soul is parched and weary, and my hands reach out and so long for the touch of heaven's love. And all seems silent.

And I cry, beg, and plead. I pray, "I need You God. I need You!" And I wonder where is the abundant flying life when I can't get on God's wings, because I can't even find His wings. Ack!

Can anyone else relate? There are days I feel like I'm flapping and floundering, whining, and whimpering. I check and double-check to see if there was something I hadn't done that I should have done. Or something I shouldn't have done that I did. I feel chewed up, mangled, spit out, beaten to a pulp and slimed. I feel guilty if I did anything or didn't do anything.

One day when I was praying, I even had a visual of God turning away, which broke my heart. I searched to see if there was some sin in my life, apologized, repented, asked for forgiveness for any and everything, and still the battle raged.

I read God's word, prayed, begged and pleaded more. And all stayed silent.

As the internal battle raged. I read the Bible, and the words fell flat. I prayed, and the prayers seemed to bounce off the ceiling. I tried to write, and the writing didn't come. I listened to sermons and read books to kick in a level of passion, but nothing seemed to really get into the heart of the matter – the soul-neediness in my heart.

I cried, whimpered, begged and pleaded. I searched through what I've learned over the years to see if I missed some truth. The heavens stayed silent, and I remained miserable.

Then I wondered if God is ever-present, why can't I always feel His presence?

In the middle of the night, I woke and remembered something about the power of believing.

Jesus mentioned He couldn't do many miracles because of a town's unbelief[5], and that without faith it is impossible to please God[6].

Which made me wonder, if I choose to believe and have faith that God is truly with me, will that make the difference?

Regardless of the silence of heaven, I need to believe God is with me because God promises He will never leave us or forsake us. Therefore, believing results in faith which results in believing. Believing is the key to receiving.

If God tells us His love is unfailing, I have to believe His love will never fail. If God says He will help us through every situation, I have to believe He is there through all situations. Even when heaven seems silent, I choose to believe.

If believing = faith, then faith results in believing.

Hebrews 11:1 Amplified version tells us, "Now faith is the assurance (the confirmation, the title deed) of the things [we] hope for, being the proof of things [we] do not see and the conviction of their reality [faith perceiving as real fact what is not revealed to the senses]."

Or to put it more plainly, The Living Bible version reads, "What is faith? It is the confident assurance that something we want is going to happen. It is the certainty that what we hope for is waiting for us, even though we cannot see it up ahead."

Even though the heavens are silent, I will believe. I will have faith, for in the faith/believing, I have the assurances of God. By choosing to believe, the power is released to keep believing.

Flying on His Wings

Therefore, I change my prayers to, *God I can't feel You right now, but I believe You are here. I believe You are here because Your Bible tells me You are with me.*

Even though I can't feel You, even though I can't tell You are here, I believe You are with me. I believe You love me. Thank You that You are here. Thank You for Your love. Thank You for who You are. Thank You for all You do. Thank You for loving me. Thank You for Your unfailing love. Thank You that You will supply all I need. Thank You that You are the answer to everything I need. Thank You Father, that even in my flailing, whining, searching, and begging, You still love me.

Something seemed to break. A crack seemed to come in the heavenlies, and my soul opened wider, and my heartbeat again with hope. For by taking a step of faith and believing (regardless of what I see or how I feel), that must please God and open my soul to receive His blessings.[78]

Just as a toddler beginning to walk has the strong arms of a loving parent holding tight, trust doesn't come until that baby believes enough to take the first solo steps. In the belief of those first steps, comes the assurance that more steps can be taken.

There is a circular truth in trusting and believing God. As I trust and believe Him, I'm blessed with more trust and belief. **The circular truth is a lifeline that reveals more lifelines.**

We are told as we draw near to God, He will draw near to us.[9] As we give, we receive. As we seek, we find. As we knock, the doors are opened.[10] As we believe, our souls find the peace, love, and presence of God we so desperately need. We need God, and we need to believe God.

Life is hard and messy, and we need to know God and His promises are true, because if we don't believe God's truth, we have nothing to stand on and nothing to sustain or carry us through the hardships of life. It's not enough to read the Bible; we have to know The God of the Bible. If we put faith in Christ to save us, we need to put faith in Him to believe Him.

As I write this, I've been struggling with headaches and migraines for a week. I don't feel God, but I'm choosing to believe God. In the silence of my needy parched soul, hope is found in believing. I will believe even in the silence of life that God is here.

Life in Christ isn't a free ride with only mountaintop experiences. Life with Christ is a roller coaster ride with hair-raising turns and screaming highs and lows. And I've found myself screaming quite often.

I SO wish life was fair, but life isn't fair because earth is screwed-up by Satan. Yet even when the battle doesn't seem winnable, we are never left defenseless, and we are not left to fight alone. Jesus warned us troubles will come but to take courage (take heart) because He has overcome the world.[11]

When Jesus promised abundant life, it wasn't a ticket out of life's problems, but a reality that Jesus will give abundant life in spite of life's problems. Battles may rage, but the final war is won. Jesus conquered sin and death, and in the end His love triumphs. Evil will be judged and punished. Truth will reign, and eternal joyful freedom will come for those who love and follow Jesus.

Jesus can empathize with our sufferings because He suffered. Jesus understands difficulties because He experienced difficulties. He will walk with us through our trials because He has been through every trial.

For thirty-three years Jesus walked on this dirt-filled earth to feel our pain and our joys. And what He didn't experience while

He lived in the flesh of man, He has experienced through our lives, and the lives of others who have gone through every trial since the beginning of time. He was there, and He is here.

When God identifies Himself as "I Am"[12], He is giving us the truth that no matter what has happened or what may happen, He is here. He is here for the pain of yesterday and the troubles of tomorrow. God is the "I Am" who is forever in your life.

If that sounded like I stepped up on my soapbox, please forgive me. But in knowing those truths, believing those truths, comes the confidence to overcome.

We don't overcome anything without overcoming something. Every day we have to choose to be overcomers and believe God.

I want to be classified as a true believer and an overcomer. I want more than the faith of a wet noodle. And yet when those wet noodle days come that leave me floundering, wimpy, and feeling all alone in a big, bad world, God's truth is the only firm foundation.

Faith has to be more than what our parents believed, or what someone else believes, more than a religion, and more than an emotional experience. Personal faith can only stand during trials when faith is backed by God's truth that has become personal.

My faith has been through the test-wringer. I've questioned and wrestled through various parts of my journey, and I wish I could tell you I've passed every test with flying colors.

There are many days I would have waved the white flag of surrender because there are many days the enemy seemed stronger, faster, and more devious than this little Buffaloe can handle.

Yet when Jesus comes into our lives, He comes into our lives bringing **His** ability. We are never left defenseless and never without hope. Christians never have to stand alone.

The truth doesn't always make life easier, but it does make life doable and winnable. By remembering that "in Christ" we are winners, we always win. We win by the forgiveness, grace, and mercy of Jesus. We win by knowing we have eternal security with an eternal joy-filled home. God is a forgiving, loving, compassionate God who guides His children along the way.

We win because God wins, and we are God's children and God **loves** His children.

God never forsakes His children. Forsake is a word with even more amazing truths. The definition of "forsake" in the Hebrew dictionary[13] is -- to fail, leave, to depart from, leave behind, let alone, neglect, to let loose, set free, let go, to be forsaken, let drop, abandon, sink down, withdraw.

Therefore, if God NEVER forsakes us, that means He won't fail us, leave us, abandon us, neglect us, leave us behind, let go of us, let us drop, or withdraw from us.

You are never forsaken by God.

Even with that wonderful knowledge, it's not easy living in a fallen world, especially when the media bombards us with EVERYTHING negative. Trying to manage our own lives is tough enough, but when we're inundated with news from around the world, all the BAD news from around the world, life gets SO hard.

Sometimes in the negatives of life, I again flounder. I run to read the Bible, and since there are those in the Bible who heard from God when they fell on their faces. Frantic to hear from God and desperate for His presence, I fall on my face.

If I'm met with silence, I run back to where I heard from God before and wait and listen. If that doesn't work, I'll get on my knees, fold my hands, and try to pray in a way that would bring God down to talk with me.

When a gnawing discontent remains, a soul-hunger for more of God's presence, I wake early and come into my office, read books, read scripture, and pray, seeking, wanting, longing for more of God.

I read of saints of old who met with God after a certain experience, so I try to recreate *that* experience.

Then I realize I'm trying to box God into an emotional experience, in effect worshipping the experiences instead of worshiping God.

In desperation to find an emotional-high connection, that feeling of feeling God's presence, have I not idolized the feeling and my emotions, instead of idolizing God?

Am I worshiping an emotional experience instead of worshiping God in spite of the lack of emotion? Am I trying so hard to fly that I can't see the shadow of His wings?

In my desperate clinging and clawing to get to God, I forget that God is ever-present. I don't feel God, so my mind tells me God isn't there in spite of His promises that He is ever-present. I find the more I meditate on what I lack, or think I lack, or focus on the evil in this world, the more the focus has been removed from the all-sufficiency of God and the truth of His promises.

Exhausted from running, doing, and trying to recreate a feeling or experience, I figuratively collapse against God's chest.

In other words, I collapse like an exhausted toddler who has had a tizzy fit and doesn't have an ounce of strength left. Whimper...

Oh my, I realize I just wrote *I collapsed against God's chest*. Is such a thought even possible? How could I, a mere mortal, have the audacity to lean against the chest of God?

An amazing verse in John 21:20 gives insight into the heart of God. John, the beloved disciple, leans against the chest of Jesus.[14] Jesus, the God-man, the Son of God, was approachable and touchable.[15]

Jesus allowed intimacy and closeness from His disciples and other people. Jesus took little children into His arms and blessed them.[16]

Jesus touched the lame, the poor, the diseased, the outcasts and those deemed untouchable. Jesus, our Savior, God-in-flesh, brought a hands-on relationship to a fallen world.

Jesus allowed John to lean on His chest, and as a follower of Jesus, we are given the same invitation. Wow!

God is the one who longs for intimacy with you. God through His Son, Jesus invites you to lean against His chest.

I love the New Living Translation of Psalm 27:8 "My heart has heard you say, 'Come and talk with me.' And my heart responds, 'Lord, I am coming'" (Psalm 27:8, NLT).

The verse is an invitation from The Creator of the universe. Amazing, isn't it?

God calls? God wants to talk with me and you? Really?

When you are desperate for God's presence, it's Him calling to you to come to His presence. **God is The One who calls.**

Our souls are made to crave God, because we are created by God for fellowship with God, and that offer of fellowship is as intimate as resting against His chest.

I'm grateful I can come to God as I am, with my fears and frailties, my brokenness, and lack of understanding.

We can come to God because He called.

We can come to Him knowing He is the one who will bring understanding and walk with us through what we don't understand. We can come to God, not because we're good enough to come to Him, but because **He** is the one who made the invitation.

God's love isn't reserved only for the "good" people. Christ loved us enough to die for us all while we were still sinners.[17]

God's love is amazing, and not one of us is good enough to receive it, and not one of us is too bad to receive it. God's grace is BIG enough for us all.

Don't think for a minute you've fallen too far from God's mercy and love, or you are so good you don't need God's mercy and love. We are all in need of a Savior, and that Savior (Jesus) can fill every need.

Christ's love doesn't hinge on you cleaning up your act before you come to Him. He opens nail-scarred hands to receive all who will come – prostitutes, murderers, liars, adulterers, haughty people, thieves ... and those are just a few of the people named in the Bible who were transformed by God's grace to be listed in the hall of faith.[18]

Jesus reaches out to pick us up from the slime pits where we live. I've been in the slime. I've fallen face-flat into sin. I'm most embarrassed by the gunk I crawled into on my own. I'd much rather everyone notice all the bad stuff others have done to me.

I can point to the long list of hardships and try to justify my actions, but my choices were my choices. Even if they were based on something in the past, they were my choices. Yet God continued to love.

Even though God knows everything, He continues to love. And I want and need someone who won't lie or cheat or walk out on me, who adores me, who will listen when I need to talk, who will be there when I call, and loves me enough to die for me.

I want and need a forever love, a love that will never fail. I found that love in God. And His love is available to **all** who will come to Him. God's love is available for you.

God's love was with me in the nights crying from pain, sobbing from the evil touches of others, screaming from surgeries, whimpering in bed with a raging fever from a blood infection, or running back to Him covered in my own sin. God continued (and continues) to love.

I'm broken, messy, and needy, and God loves the broken, messy, and needy.

No matter how wrecked a life, God's love and restoration are available.

I have friends whose lives were absolute messes, and yet God found them and loved them. My friend, Marlyn, called me a "lifer" because I was raised in the church. She said she was a "rimmer" because she grew up on the "toilet-seat of life." (Her childhood was spent living over a bar.)

Marlyn watched and studied to see if I lived what I professed, and as our friendship grew, she confessed she wasn't even sure how to pray, so we began to pray together. We prayed over the phone or through email on the computer. I would type in a prayer, and then she would type in her own.

She learned to pray, and in the process, she taught me how to pray deeper than I had ever known. The teacher became the student as her prayers transcended my church jargon. Her simple prayers were of an adult who came to Christ as a broken child. No request was too small or too large for herself, her husband, and her young daughter.

When pancreatic cancer struck, Marlyn stuck with Christ. She went deeper and further in her faith. Her prayers took on holy ground as the focus narrowed on the important things in life. There is nothing shallow when death is standing at the door.

Marlyn battled through her fears and doubts, and her faith stood firm even when she couldn't stand. Even when she couldn't feel God beyond the pain and suffering, she believed and trusted God.

She became bold for Christ and witnessed what God had done in her life to other patients and doctors. Marlyn lived well in her dying days.

Marlyn's faith in God, her testimony, her walk, and her prayers laid a beautiful groundwork for her husband to see and find the God she loved. Before she flew home to be with Jesus, her unbelieving husband became a believer.

I miss Marlyn. I miss her scrutiny of my Christianity. I miss her honesty to get me to step away from the Christianese platitudes, for they were hollow until I allowed the truth to get soul deep.

Marlyn came to God with honesty, and honesty is what God desires.[19]

I don't have to whitewash my prayers, pretend I have everything figured out, or even hide my hurt and questions. God already knows every thought, therefore why try to pretend my thoughts are better than what I'm thinking?

There is nothing more precious than an honest friendship where you can tell someone your heart and know your heart is safe. God is honest friendship wanting honest friendship. God meets us where we are.

God has found me in the depths of agony and in the depths of wrong living. I could honestly come to Him with my hurts and come to Him when I was covered in the garbage of life. Through God's grace, He welcomed me into His arms.

He welcomed me in spite of my questions, in spite of my stubbornness, and in spite of my willful disobedience. God welcomed me when I came to Him and admitted what I was feeling, admitted my failures, and even admitted I was totally clueless as to why I did what I did.

God wants us to come to Him because He wants a relationship with us. Jesus told His followers we aren't just servants, we're friends,[20] and friends want to spend time together.

I love spending time with my friends, and God invites us to that same kind of relational living.

There is a brief mention of a man in the Bible named Enoch. The Bible tells us

Enoch "walked with God" and then God took him straight into heaven.[21] No death, no suffering is mentioned, just a one-way ticket straight to heaven. I would love that. Yes, please!

The Bible doesn't give insight how Enoch accomplished this achievement. If the Bible had listed out Enoch's daily routine, would I have started trying to do things exactly like Enoch? And if I had, would I have in effect become someone who worshiped Enoch's way instead of God's way? Yes, probably.

There is something beautifully unconfining about Enoch. He wasn't mentioned because of his accomplishments and huge ministry, but because of his relationship with God.

Enoch walked with God. I'm not sure what all that statement entails, but I think it means we don't have to be so concerned about how our time with God is done, but where our focus remains. If our center of attention is on God, then we will walk with God.

Relationship is key and takes away the confines of what others (or the world) thinks our relationship with God should look like.

Experiences with God are moment-by-moment, day-by-day, changing, and growing. Jesus moved among humanity, talking, healing, walking, going, stopping to pray, and touching lives in different ways every different day. And as we move forward, we can talk, walk (even if bed-ridden), listen, pray, and touch lives that God sends our way.

David approached God in honesty, and I think that's one of the reasons God called David a man after His own heart. David is transparent in his struggles; he is real with God because He knows God is real. David pours out his anger and frustration. He asks God questions and makes suggestions to God that still make me uncomfortable (see Psalm 69).

David didn't mince words; he wanted his enemies wiped off the earth. He was a warrior, yet at times he lived in caves, was afraid, and ran for his life. He cried out, didn't understand, and didn't know why God brought him to those difficulties. Yet David circled back to believe and trusted God regardless of what he felt or experienced.

The times I'm afraid, hurt, and wandering through life, I cling to the Psalms and read them in the quiet moments, or read them out loud. Psalm 42 and Psalm 43 speak of the desperate longings of the soul, and I read, underline, and pray them to God. The Psalms give voice to sorrow. They are a lifeline to again find life.

When difficulties come, it's easy to blame God or run from Him. During those times, I have to not only buckle my seatbelt, I have to lash myself to God. I have to believe in God's goodness even when the world is so bad and so evil.

Paul says we live by faith, not by sight (2 Corinthians 5:7). However, the Christian faith isn't sightless belief; it is spiritual-sighted belief in The Truth because The Truth lives in our hearts. Jesus comes into our lives and gives us the capability for further belief.

So if you want to fly, you've got to believe you can fly. Or perhaps more accurately, you've got to believe with God you will fly.

God calls the most unlikely people to follow Him, often choosing the ones who aren't the smartest, strongest, or richest. [22]

The world tells us only the strong survive, only the beautiful are chosen, and only those with super-powers become super-heroes. However, God chooses Clark Kents instead of Supermen, and then turns

Clark Kents into Supermen.

Gideon was the youngest from the "least" tribe, and yet God turned him into a warrior and deliverer.

David was a lowly shepherd turned into giant-slayer and king.

Lowly fishermen became fishers of men and turned the world upside down.

God takes nobodies and makes them somebodies in His kingdom. He is in the job of transforming us into the image of His Son. Don't ever say you aren't qualified. "Not that we are adequate in ourselves to consider anything as coming from ourselves, but **our adequacy is from God**" (2 Corinthians 3:5, NASB). (That's encouraging good news!)

God doesn't base what He can do on our strength, but through His might. No army is too big; nothing stands in our way that is mightier than God.

God's view is opposite of the worldview. You aren't what others have said about you. You aren't a label. You aren't even what you think about yourself. Your true identity is God's child.

As His child, you have the power of God within you. "Now to Him who is able to do **far more abundantly beyond all that we ask or think, according to the power that**

works within us, to Him be the glory in the church and in Christ Jesus to all generations forever and ever. Amen" (Ephesians 3:20-21, NASB).

With God, the least becomes the greatest, and the last becomes the first. Jesus sacrificed His life to give new life to all who believe. Christians exchange their lives to become new creations—sons and daughters of The King of kings.

As sons and daughters of The King, we are given access to The Throne and power to live, equipped to go through whatever comes next.

Whatever has happened in your life, whatever you face, God has equipped you. You are never without what you need to recover or to move forward. Since God is here now and will be with you on every step of the journey, His provision is already there to equip you for each and every need and challenge.

That phone call that rocked your world, that flood that washed away your home, the destroying fire, the pain of the past, and the suffering of the future -- nothing is too much for God. Nothing catches Him by surprise, and nothing will come that God has not already equipped you to go through.

The same is true for those you love or those who you hear about on the news or social media or through friends and family. Whatever happens in their life, whatever they face, God has equipped them.

The Greek definition of equipping is to be complete, furnishing, perfecting. Equipping is a mending, arranging, adjusting, strengthening, completing to be perfected through the all-encompassing power of Jesus Christ.

God's equipping isn't just barely enough. God equips in abundance.[23]

I think of God's equipping as a backpack of supplies we are given at birth. Our supply pack is stuffed with everything needed for life's journey. And through God's equipping is sufficiency to be sufficient through God.

The Greek meaning of sufficiency is a perfect condition of life in which no aid or support is needed, sufficiency of the necessities of life, a mind contented with its lot, contentment. [24]

When you look at your past, your daily life, the future that may come, remember God's equipping, abundant sufficiency is with you every step of the way.

You are equipped for the next year, month, week, day, and minute. God supplies you with enough grace, enough strength, enough mercy, and enough love. God is with your every breath, every step, every need, and through everything. Rest content friends, you are equipped. [25]

God doesn't base what He can do on our strength, but through His might. Nothing stands in our way with more power than God.

Another cool fact is that you are gifted. In Christ, we all receive one gift after another, different gifts according to the grace given to each of us (John 1:16 Romans 12:6).

In Matthew 25, Jesus relates the story about the wealthy owner who was leaving on a trip and gave his servants talents.

In the same way you too are gifted, you are given talents, you have a purpose and a place on this planet. God-given gifts don't wear out or expire, and they don't have a retirement date.[26]

What we are given remains to be used to glorify God now and for eternity. The wonderful news is, God's gifts come with a bonus of bounce-back blessings. The more we give, the more we receive.

Remember "Jesus has the power of God, by which <u>he has given us everything we</u>

<u>need to live and to serve God</u>. We have these things because we know him. Jesus called us by his glory and goodness. Through these he gave us the very great and precious promises. With these gifts you can share in God's nature" (2 Peter 1:3-4a, NCV) (underline, mine).

Buckle your seatbelt. Through Christ you are empowered with God's power, sufficiently gifted and equipped to fly through every moment of life.

Baggage Handling

A senior executive of a large corporation was given his own corporate jet. The man commissioned the airplane to be outfitted to his specifications, and he didn't just want a standard plane, he wanted the best. Premium materials were ordered to outfit the interior with the finest money could buy.

Unfortunately, the man didn't take into account the weight of his high-dollar items. After the modifications were completed, his jet was not deemed flight-worthy with the added mass.

I'm sure the executive didn't intend to only drive around an airport runway. Unfortunately in the same way, there are many people relegated to sitting at the gate of life never even pushing back, others driving around runways, and some flying but only a few feet off the ground.

Satan heaps on fear, worry, and shame to keep as many grounded as possible. Burdens are carried, weighing down and hindering flight.

The Tower says we're cleared for takeoff, but we can't fly until we remove the things that need to be removed. I've been grounded many times. I've tried to cover over inadequacies, insecurities, fears, and worries by stuffing so much in my baggage compartments I can't get off the ground. Fortunately, God is teaching me to eject the baggage and trash the trash.

I found a pair of jeans which had been stuffed in the back of my closet. Without a moment's hesitation, I put them on. I wore them while I worked in my office, went out to lunch, and met later with several friends.

About seven that evening, when I bent over to check inside the oven, one of my friends pointed out I had a rip in my jeans. Not just a little tiny rip, but a shredded, humiliating, **huge** gap in the seat of my pants. Ack! Humiliation galore!

Then I remembered I had originally put the pants aside hoping one day to apply a patch. I even recalled my sweet husband suggesting I throw them out because the rip was so large.

But noooooo, I thought I knew better.

Whimper. I should have listened.

Which makes me wonder how many times do I not fly free because of something in the past, some trash I haven't trashed? If I haven't allowed God's healing, the baggage from the past weighs me down with ever-bulging baggage compartments.

How many times have I worn an identity that should be thrown out, wearing my "old self" instead of walking as a new creation in Christ? And how many times have I worn a label someone else gave me instead of the truth of who I am in Christ?

I look back on my life and cringe at the sinful, stupid mistakes. Strolling down memory lane leaves me totally mortified. God clearly laid out the guidelines, and yet I ran in the wrong direction.

There have been times I've opened my mouth, and words spilled out that weren't helpful or uplifting, sentences freefalling and smashing on the ground before the common-sense parachute took over.

Wouldn't it be wonderful to go back and get a "do over", a rewind, or retake?

If given the opportunity to redo my past, I wouldn't have acted "that" way. I wouldn't have talked "that" way. I wouldn't have done "that" I wouldn't have said "that." Oh my goodness, if only mistakes could be changed.

I would love to go back and apologize to all the people I've hurt, said stupid things to, or have seen me in my failures. I'd love to scrape up the mistakes, or words off the ground, and flip them over to a new opportunity.

Fortunately, we can run back to God and ask for forgiveness. "If we confess our sins, He is faithful and just to forgive us our sins and to cleanse us from all unrighteousness" (1 John 1:9, NKJV).

Within God's love, forgiveness has already been applied and the past erased. God never throws sin back in our faces, because God not only forgives—He forgets.

Our memories remain so we can learn and grow, help others, and hopefully keep us from stumbling again in that direction.

God's unfailing love picks us up from the mess we've made, wipes us off, and gives another opportunity to do better with His help and guidance.

God's grace is as high as the heavens are above the earth. And our sins are removed as far as the east is from the west.[27]

If we want to fly, we've got to eject the

baggage and move forward in the grace, newness, freedom, and love of Jesus.

The truth is, if Jesus sets us free, we are free.[28] If we are believers in Jesus, whatever is in our past is in the past and the new has come. [29]

The truth is, Christ died for us while we were **still** sinners. God put a rescue plan before we were "good enough" or did the "right" things. The rescue was in place while we were still a mess.

The truth is, grace is simple, and simply amazing because of the amazing sacrifice of Jesus. In knowing God's truth, we can eject our baggage.

Baggage comes in a variety of colors, shapes, and sizes. Insecurity is one bag I've dragged around for years. When I was a teenager, I moaned and whined and complained about my insecurities to a friend. I had gone through a mutant phase that lasted for years and even though I was now looking somewhat human, I still couldn't get over the feelings of not being accepted or looking like the rest of the in-crowd.

I bemoaned my plight to my friend. Poor me, poor me, poor me. Poor me! Whimper. Sob. Whiiiiiiinnnnne.

My friend's response? "You are so stuck-up!"

What? Ouch!

My friend's blunt comment reminded me when all I think about is my insecurities and inadequacies, I am stuck-up - stuck on myself. I wasn't thinking of others and not considering anyone else but myself. I was stuck-up in the attitude of ungratefulness, shallowness, and the rut of self-infatuation. Bummer.

Insecurity is a lack of confidence not only in ourselves but in God. Insecurities stick us up above everyone else, above God's truth, causing us to miss His blessings of God-confidence, joy, love, and peace. Eternal safety and confidence can't be found in something that isn't eternal.

> Insecurity = Self focus.
> Security = God focus.

Unfortunately, it's much easier to focus on me and my needs because I know me and my needs. And my needs get really, really needy.

In the insecurity mode, "me" gets rather bossy, whiny, clingy, and demanding. And then Myself and I gangs up on Me and the fight gets all consuming and all-encompassing and turns my life outside in. And the only focus is on me and my problems, my concerns, my life, my situation, my job, my family, my ... oh my, oh me!

Do you also have problems with me? I knew it! Me is a problem!

Life gets wrapped up in me that I can't live life because me is in the way of life. The Me trap, traps me, and the self-focus battle rages with the self which is always involved in picturing selfies about everything that deals with the self of me.

Ack, I'm out of rest and can't find peace when everything is about me. However, if I turn the focus off me and onto God, I find the reality of the promise of Isaiah 26:3, "You will keep him in perfect peace, whose mind is stayed on You, because he trusts in You" (NKJV).

Peace comes by turning the focus on The One who is peace and The One trustworthy for every little needs of my "me" self.

We find our way when we look to Jesus who is The Way. Each day and every moment we have to make a choice whom we will serve. As for me? I'm gonna tell me to keep my mind on The One who can make my mind mind. I'm going to serve God instead of me.[30]

When I choose to believe (truly believe) God created me, knows me, loves me, and will never fail me, insecurity fades away when the focus is properly adjusted to center on our BIG, AMAZING, loving God!

Once we get ourselves out of the way, God can move in wonderful ways. The Christian life is not about what we can get, but what we can give – our heart, our mind, and our soul to Christ. Dying to self is taking Me off the throne of my life and acknowledging Christ as King of my life.

When we give our all to Jesus, we receive His all to be who we were created to be and receive His abundant life. As we surrender ourselves to Christ, lay down ourselves to Christ, we are created new in Christ.

Surrender of self = self-sacrifice that yields unfettered, undeterred, unhindered free-flowing movement of God's Spirit, power, and strength.

Surrender is freedom.

Surrender is a leaning into God, a relinquishing of the past, today, and the future. It is a prying off of fingers, letting go,

Flying on His Wings

and surrendering.

One night while lying in bed, I felt led to raise my hands, to let go of everything in absolute trust. I hesitated, and really struggled with God's request. Because even in the safety of my own room, with my sweet husband snoozing peacefully beside me, God's request was huge. Because there were times in my life when my hands were immobilized by attackers. And the thought of raising my hands, of not being in control, terrified me.

I knew God wasn't just requesting something for that night, He was asking me to let go of the fears of the past and the fears of the future. Cautiously, slowly, I surrendered and raised my hands.

In that moment, God gave me a sweet visual. I was under His wings as He flew. And when I raised my hands, He flipped me in joy to His back, and we flew swiftly to the heavens.

And I found the truth that whatever is surrendered to God is replaced with more of Him which leads to more of His joy. The surrendered life to God leads to a life of joy with God.

Surrendering allows a freefall knowing the fall will lead to death of self which leads to a new life in Christ. Hidden in Christ, our fears are put to death because we are eternally safe in Christ. We surrender earthly weak power and human strength to receive the almighty power and strength of our all-powerful God.

Surrendering to God always comes with amazing blessings.

I had flown to Houston for a speaking event, and my flight was provided by a wonderful couple affiliated with the church's women's retreat ministry (waving thanks to Kelly and Jay-Jay).

To my delight, I found because of his generosity, I was given the same frequent-flyer status he had while flying. His upper-level status gave me the ability to check in a preferred line and walk through unencumbered and free without worry or hassle.

Because of the merciful generosity and grace of Jesus, we are given full-access freedom to stand before our Holy God.

Unfortunately, we can block God's blessings and our own freedom by not surrendering a bag that many carry – the baggage of offense.

With all the evil in the world, it's easy to get offended – offended at injustice, offended at pain we suffer or someone else suffers. It's easy to be offended at people for their actions and easy to be offended that God didn't stop the evil.

If we pick up the bag of offense for ourselves or someone else, the more that offense is picked up, the bigger and heavier it becomes.

John the Baptist's entire ministry was built on preparing and making the way for Jesus. His life was dedicated to preaching and pointing to the Messiah. When he saw Jesus, John declared, "Behold, the Lamb of God who takes away the sin of the world!" (John 1:29, NASB).

John baptized Jesus and knew Jesus as Messiah. Yet when John found himself in prison, he questioned, wondered, and didn't understand. Would prison be the fate for the one who proclaimed Christ had come into the world?

Through John's followers he sent word to Jesus asking, "Are You the Expected One, or shall we look for someone else?" (John 11:2)

In the midst of heartache and tragedy, human nature questions, wonders, and doesn't understand. How can those things happen? Were we incorrect in what we thought? God, are you still in control?

And the enemy (who is behind **all** the evil) taunts, if God was good, He wouldn't allow *that* to happen.

Jesus didn't rebuke John but sent a gentle reminder of all the things Jesus had done proving He truly was the Messiah.[31] Jesus responded, "And blessed (happy, fortunate, and to be envied) is he who takes no offense at Me and finds no cause for stumbling in or through Me and is not hindered from seeing the Truth" (Matthew 11:6, AMP).

The fact that John was in prison was offensive. John's suffering and beheading were offensive. We can be offended at injustice but need to be careful not to be offended at God. (Why aren't we offended at Satan for the horrible, terrible things **he** incites and institutes?)

Offenses are a stumbling block that can cause us to stumble in our faith and keep us from seeing the truth.

Offenses and bitterness defile many and blocks (shortens) the grace of God. Bitterness chokes grace and mercy, defiles one generation after another, and spoils with ill-will, destruction, and sorrow.[32]

Offended wounds ooze with

defensiveness that blocks opportunities for healing.

Offended wounds create hardened soul-scars that won't allow the ointment of God's tender touch.

Bitterness destroys lives, families, cities, and communities. Offended wounds infect souls with the pus of bitterness, anger, and rage.

Don't allow offended wounds to stay in your life. Don't allow a root of bitterness or become bitter because of what happened to someone else (or is happening).

Drop your offenses at the foot of the cross. Let Jesus have anything that has offended you and anything that causes bitterness.

Even though you don't understand, even when life doesn't make sense, trust God. Don't let the enemy block the free-flowing life Jesus gives. Don't let your abundant life be choked off by ingratitude, anger, or bitterness. Sin crouches at the door, and the devil is always looking for a foothold. The enemy wants to block the flow and block our fruit for God's Kingdom.

Forgiveness and blessings pour forth healing. Trust and faith pour forth restoration. Believing in God's goodness restores hope. Knowing, truly knowing, God gives joy and encouragement.

Trust God with the things in your past that caused you to be offended. Give Him your anger. Praise Him and let His blessings flow to you and through you.

If your friend, loved one, or even a stranger is suffering remember God's grace and healing is also available for them. God doesn't need to share grace with you for that person's injuries. God doesn't need to give grace to you that belongs to them.

Grace is freely given for each person, each need, each circumstance, each hardship, and each situation. Just as a good doctor won't prescribe pain medication to you for someone else's injuries, God will give each according to their needs.

God will grant us grace to go through our difficulties -- grace for our difficulties, not grace for someone else's difficulties. When we take on another's difficulties as ours, we will not receive <u>their</u> grace.

Focus on what the Lord has done for you, not what the enemy has done to you. Don't build memorials or idols to the enemy, build memorials to God. Don't idolize your grief or the grief of others.

God's heart bleeds at man's sinful

nature. God's perfect nature is love. He cares. God not only created emotions, He also feels every emotion we feel. When the Bible tells us of God's tender mercies, He is tender. He is kind, compassionate, and loving toward all He has made.

God's heart bleeds with you as you cry. His arms long to hold you close. And someday very soon, He will punish the evildoers, He will set every captive free, and He will wipe away every tear. Trust God with life's injuries and suffering.

The other day something from my past came to mind, and I grieved. I mourned what was lost and what could never be regained. And yet I felt guilty, so I asked God if it was okay to be sad about that situation.

I felt His Spirit whisper in mine that it was okay to grieve but not to make the grief an idol.

God grants freedom to grieve and freedom to heal. However, if our grief is idolized above the freedom and healing offered by God, the enemy has gained a foothold.

Satan would love for us all to be stuck in the pain of the past, never moving forward, and never allowing God to heal. The only one worth idolizing is God. He is the only One worthy of our worship. Worship is another key to freedom, because as we worship God our countenance is raised to look above the grief, above the attacks of the enemy, and into the comforting arms of our loving God.

God's comforting love is deep enough, rich enough, and wide enough for any loss and any grief. Through the grace, mercy, and love of our Savior we find the healing for our soul wounds.

One morning I felt a tug on my soul as though God's unseen hand was asking me to spend time with Him. I knelt in front of our fireplace with my Bible.

While I was praying, I sensed a need to polish our coffee table. I'm easily distracted, but this seemed different. The table looked fine, yet there was an almost playful thought that this urge was more than a cleaning project.

I started rubbing the wood with polish and a cloth, and as I worked several truths became clear. The wood is beautiful but the imperfections add character. The knots, rings, and scars formed by growth, environment, hardships, and trials, brought beauty to the wood. The imperfections add a richness and glow.

Scars tell of the journey.

I have scars from my head to my toes. Some scars have funny stories, some do not. They all changed me.

Life leaves scars, internal and external marks of what we have been through. Those scars are precious. They are proof of survival during the fires of life. Scars glow with the testimonies of God's faithfulness.

No matter how deep the scars, God's love runs deeper, and His love turns everything into beauty. Scars tell the most precious story–the story of Jesus and His sacrifice for you. His scars prove His love for you. Jesus' scars prove that your life was worth the suffering to save your life.

In the suffering and beyond the suffering, the heart of God beats tender with healing, hope, and restoration.

The most often quoted example of suffering is found in the book of Job. Although Job was a righteous man, he lost his children, his home, his livelihood, and his health.

Through all the hardships, all his questions, wonderings, and pain, he cried for God to answer him and help him understand. For thirty-seven long chapters God is silent.

When God finally answers, He never explains the reasons behind Job's sufferings.

Job's response? "I have heard of You by the hearing of the ear; but now my eye sees You" (Job 42:5, NASB). Job didn't get his answer to the question of his suffering; he came to a greater knowledge of God. He saw more of God.

Trials and suffering strip away earthly thinking. If we will allow, if we will look to God, we will see more of God. The righteous suffer and yet will come through with the nourishment of a solid Gospel, the truth of God's presence, the strength of His arms, and the blessings that wait on the other side.

Nothing is wasted by God, and through all you have suffered, all you have seen and experienced, there is an amazing beauty of finding more of God.

Don't give up. The beauty is coming.

God takes the broken places and makes them whole. He heals, sustains, helps, and saves. His goodness, mercy, grace, justice, and tender love are waiting. Allow Him to comfort you as you grieve.

Place your grief in His strong, loving arms, worship Him, and allow His comfort to wash over you. No matter what you are going through, God is with you and bring you safely home.

Within the book of John, we find a story about a man who had been an invalid for thirty-eight years. He and many others, the blind, lame, and paralyzed lay waiting by the pool of Bethesda.

The Bethesda pool was no ordinary pool. People believed the water would occasionally be stirred by the touch of an angel, and the first one in would be healed. Day after day those needing a miracle would watch and wait.

Then Jesus walked into his life and asked, "Do you wish to get well?"[33]

The man at the pool was in the masses, yet all alone. Did family and friends take him there when the illness first struck, or had they cared for a time and then lost hope?

Jesus didn't address everyone. He addressed this man. I find it interesting Jesus asked such a question. The guy had been an invalid for thirty-eight years; wouldn't he *want* to be well? I think I would have said YES! I would have begged and pleaded for any help offered.

However, the man answered he had no one to put him into the pool, and someone else always would get in before him.[34] The man focused on his own weakness and own inabilities, perhaps he was even comfortable with his uncomfortable life. Resigned to his fate, that no one was there to help him, the man never answered Jesus' question.

The man answers out of his lack.

Jesus answers with unmerited grace.

"Jesus said to him, 'Rise, take up your bed and walk'" (John 5:8, NKJV).

When Jesus walked into the man's life, he was given the option to get well. The choice was his. The man couldn't heal himself, but he could respond to the words Jesus spoke. And he did. "And immediately the man was made well, took up his bed, and walked" (John 5:8-9, NKJV).

We cannot always choose what happened to us or what is happening in our lives, but we have an option how we respond and what we will do in our present life.

Refusing to release our pain, infirmities, painful memories, or wrongs committed against us, we become like the invalid at the pool complaining that no one is ever there to carry us, even as the Great Physician stands with His hand outstretched asking "Do you want to get well?"

The enemy wants you to stay down, stay in your unforgiveness, your bitterness, and stay in the midst of your painful past. Yet Jesus says, "Rise and walk."

If we believe Jesus Christ took on our sins, was raised from the dead, and offers eternal life, why the hesitation to believe God can heal us from our past?

One day I used the trimmer to prepare the yard before my sweet husband mowed. While working, I heard a pop, felt a sharp sting in my lower leg, but couldn't see any damage through my jeans.

A few minutes later, I felt a trickle of something wet from that area. I lifted my pant leg to see blood where a shard of plastic string had shot through my jeans, and impaled my leg above the ankle. Yikes and ack!

The string was stuck deep enough a tug didn't even get it to budge. I hurried to find my husband to help. When we couldn't get it out with gentle pulls, I wasn't too thrilled with how hard the removal might become.

Now I had several choices to make. I could leave the string embedded in my leg, allow it to fester and become infected, or have it removed to allow healing.

When my husband grabbed a pair of needle-nose pliers, I found strength to pull even harder. With a pop (and probably a scream), the evil instrument was extracted from my leg. The process wasn't fun, but the healing could now begin.

A small piece of trimmer string seems harmless until it's imbedded in skin.

How many barbs are stuck in your soul?
Healing is needed when wounded.
Forgiveness allows healing.

Take the barbs, the quills, the shrapnel, and embedded wounds to the Great Physician. Allow Him full access, and the freedom will be yours, the healing will be yours, and the restoration will be yours.

Man says some things are just too difficult to overcome, but nothing is impossible for God.

Man says there is no hope for restoration, but God is The God of restorations.

Man says nothing good can come from some things, God says He will turn **all** things to the good for those who love Him and are called to His purposes.

Man points to defeat, God **is** victory.

Believe and move forward. Drop the past at the empty tomb. Our Savior is not dead. Jesus is alive, and His saving grace brings the dead back to life.

You are the one who can make the

difference as you allow God full access to untangle what has entangled you.

Hebrews 12:1-2 and 1 Corinthians 9:24 tell us to run the race to win the prize, laying aside anything that hinders so we can run with endurance the race set before us, as we fix our eyes on Jesus.

I visualize a huge running track. Several huge groups of people are clumped together, lots of smaller groups move in unison, but most runners are quietly running alone. There are even a few who sit in the track and trip up other runners. Others sit faced forward, and others are sitting faced backwards, blocking and hindering other runners. Occasionally someone will stop and lift up the squatters, gently prodding and encouraging them forward.

I think I've been in all those categories. At times I've sat starting backward at my past, unable to move forward, even perhaps hindering others as I bemoaned all the bad things that have happened. Even when I stood on my feet, I still didn't quite make it into the race. Often I've tried to connect with a large group, looking at people for healing and answers instead of looking to Jesus.

Yet when I fixed my eyes on Jesus,

when I focused squarely on Him, then I could run with abandon, leave the past behind, and run in my own lane, free and unhindered.

So my questions for all of us...

Are we so preoccupied with the past that we are sitting and squatting instead of facing forward and running? Do we hinder or encourage other runners? Are we stumbling over the past instead of running free? Do we look at the other runners, the other groups, instead of looking to Jesus? Are we running our individual race, the race God has for us? Will we fix our eyes squarely on Jesus and run with abandon?

Let's run free, friends. Let's run to win!

Remember the only thing that can truly hinder you is *you*. The enemy might try to trip you up, throw obstacles in your way, and get you off track, but your inner person is never hindered.

Your soul can always stand. Regardless of your circumstances, your past, your current life, who you live with, work with, or where you live, you are unhindered in Christ.

Stand for Christ even if you can't walk. Stand in awe of God. Stand in the reality that you are free in Christ. Stand firm knowing

God will guide you. Stand in the rest of God. Stand in the freedom of Christ.

Stand firm in the knowledge you are loved by God with an unfailing love. Stand, sit, kneel, and/or walk in prayer. Stand in praise. Stand strong. Stand firm against the enemy. Stand firm in God's truth. Stand firm in your faith.

Remember, "It was for freedom that Christ set us free; therefore, keep standing firm ..." (Galatians 5:1, NASB). Always keep your soul standing firm in Christ.

Christ's freedom is available for each of us. Paul told us to "accept one another, just as Christ also accepted us to the glory of God" (Romans 15:7, NASB).

My friend has a tainted past. Jesus changed who she is now; her past has been washed clean and replaced with a new opportunity to begin a new life in Him. The past remains unchanged, but through Jesus' forgiveness, she is changed. Even when she told her husband and new friends about her past, they continued to love and accept her.

Unfortunately, ancient history, memories, and past perceptions cloud the vision of those who knew her in her younger days. Why do they refuse to see who she is now and who she strives to be through her

Savior?

My friend is not the only one with this problem. How often do past failures cloud our vision? The past pollutes the present, which stagnates growth and change. We see what we choose to see in ourselves and others.

God sees the good in each of us, so much so, that Jesus died for us even while we were sinners.

We all require second chances. Beethoven's teacher said he was hopeless as a composer.

Albert Einstein didn't talk until he was three, didn't write until he was seven, and was termed mentally slow and unsociable by his teacher.

Saul was a Christian hater and murderer.

David was an adulterer and a murderer.

Peter denied Christ.

Rahab was a prostitute.

What if they had not been given another chance?

God is the God of second chances. He asks that we love as He loves. "A new command I give you: Love one another. As I have loved you, so you must love one another" (John 13:34, NIV).

God's love is for us all. Every. Single. One. Of. Us.

That even means you. Through Christ's forgiveness, you are given a new opportunity for a new life.

And the amazing cool thing about God's love is that His love is patient, kind, doesn't envy, doesn't boast, isn't proud. Isn't rude or self-seeking, isn't easily angered, <u>and keeps no record of wrongs</u>. God's love doesn't delight in evil but rejoices with the truth. God's love always protects, always trusts, <u>always hopes</u>, and always perseveres. [35]

Let others drop their baggage at the foot of the Cross, and remember to drop yours.

We are called to love with God's love, which doesn't just mean loving other people, that even means loving ourselves. Look through God's eyes when you look at others and when you look in the mirror, and I promise you a new look at life. You are not what you did in the past, not what someone else did to you in the past. The past is past.

Who you are in Christ is a new creation, given mercies every morning from a gracious God. Every day the old has gone, and the new has come. Forget the past by giving the past to The One who can heal any past. Run the race of today by fixing your eyes on Jesus.

You are a child of the King. Live today knowing who you are in Christ. Don't think your sin is too bad or too big to be forgiven. God's lovingkindness never stops and His compassions never fail.[36]

There are many who have suffered, many who have sinned, many who thought their past or their sins would keep them from living a full life. Yet the Bible and history are full of examples of those who failed, went through terrible difficulties, and yet lived amazing productive Christian lives.

Don't sit on the sidelines or allow the enemy to sidetrack you. Press on, press past the past, and reach forward to Jesus.

From a sound sleep, the thought came at 4:00 in the morning. "*I know what you did.*"

I woke with a start as the memories of my past sins attacked and left me reeling.

Embarrassment and sorrow grew until I remembered, **I know what He did**! Jesus offered forgiveness, grace, mercy. When I ran to Him with my sins, He cleansed me and washed me white as snow.

I remember what others did -- my innocence gone, and my heart and soul shredded. Yet I remember and know what

Jesus did – He mended, restored, renewed, and recovered what the enemy had stolen.

When Satan taunts you with your past, remind him what Jesus has done!

Whatever has happened in your past, whatever you have done, whatever someone else has done to you, Jesus has done what needs to be done to give you a new hope and a new future.

So let's throw off the past, throw off the enemy attacks with God's truth, and throw off anything weighing us down and remember we are free in Christ.

We visited the Oregon Trail Interpretive Center where life-sized dioramas recreate the journey.

I'm amazed, absolutely awe-struck at those who ventured across endless, dry, hot prairie, over mountains and treacherous rivers. The trails marked by graves and heartache.

The numbers of travelers are estimated between 200,000 and 500,000. Ruts from wagon wheels remain in the landscape to this day. Can you imagine traveling six months without gas stations, coffee shops, restaurants, and a hotel? Plus, no facilities for us prim and proper ladies. Ack! Gasp, wheeze ...

Letters recorded what the travelers packed. Their choices often resulted in life or death. Cook stoves, silver, china, even pianos, littered the landscape as travelers left behind non-essential belongings.

I don't think my computer or cellphone would have made it very far. Makes me shudder. Thank goodness I don't have to travel the Oregon Trail, but it sure makes me wonder – are we holding on to things that hinder our journeys?

The writer of Hebrews tells us to strip off and throw aside anything that hinders, any unnecessary weight, and any sin that entangles, and run our race (see Hebrews 12:1).[37]

In the battle, you don't carry anything you don't need. We need to remember to eject any baggage that needs ejecting, throw off the worry weight, kick out the sin, and evict the fear.

God didn't give us the spirit of fear.[38] Did you catch the word—spirit? When we entertain "fear," we are entertaining a spirit from the enemy. The definition of fear is cowardice, craven/cringing fear, fawning fear, gnawing fear, or timidity. Eww!

Kick out fear because fear doesn't belong to God, and if we belong to God, we don't have to entertain a spirit from the other side. Throw out fear!

And please examine how you filter your view of God, life, and who you are.

During my younger days, we lived in an old farmhouse. The water supply came from a well far beyond its prime. The rusty water made it difficult to drink, as well as keeping clothing, sinks, and the bathtub clean.

Replacing the filter on the well helped but only for a short time. Sediment and rust would quickly overwhelm the system. The difficulties continued until my parents had enough money to dig a deeper well to reach a clean and clear supply of water.

Regardless of how messy your past, how messy your current situation, how overwhelming life may seem, God's clean, clear, truth filters away the rust and sediment from the enemy's lies.

Regardless of what the world and society thinks, says, or does, the only way to find the clear, clean Truth is in the truth of God's word.

Regardless of what others have said about you, pronounced about you, did to you, spoke over you ... God's truth is that you are God's beloved child and He loves you.

True freedom exists in God's truth, in the reality of who you are in Christ. Check your filter. Daily. Moment-by-moment. Your thoughts and perception are under attack.

Check, check, and double-check to make sure what you believe and what you know about yourself and others is filtered through God's freeing truth.

So who said you'll never be forgiven for that sin? Who said you've gone too far from God? Who said you'll never amount to anything? Who said you'll never be able to accomplish your goals? Who said you're all alone? Who said you aren't loving?

Don't listen to those who don't speak God's truth.

God says He is forgiving and will wash you as white as snow.

God says to return to Him and He'll wipe away your transgressions.

God says His mercies are new every morning.

God says He heals the brokenhearted.

God says nothing is impossible for Him.

God says He is faithful to complete what He started in you.

God says He will never leave you or forsake you.

God says He will love you forever.
Let's listen to God and His truth.[39]

Drop your baggage and allow others to drop their baggage. God is unlimited, His resources, power, strength, and might are inexhaustible.

Jesus grants first-class access to live in His freedom. Let's check our baggage at the foot of the cross and fly free!

Trusting The Pilot

Clouds bulged and boiled in the distance as I stared out the airplane window. My son and I were flying from Idaho to join my husband in Tennessee. Our house had sold, our belongings were on a moving truck, and we were making the final part of our journey to the Memphis area.

Sitting in my window seat I had plugged in my headphones and turned on praise music as I stared at the nighttime sky. Lightning streaked through the clouds below providing a light show as we traveled.

With bad weather in the area, the pilot had suspended any service and everyone was told to stay in their seats. Thirty minutes before our scheduled landing, the pilot announced the weather had grown too difficult to land and we were rerouted to another location where we could refuel and wait out the storms.

The plane banked to change course, and I glanced at the time and sat back continuing to pray and praise God. Nothing could be done but wait and see what would happen next.

Fifteen minutes later, the plane started it's decent. The plane bounced and shook as the turbulence grew, but then the pilot made another turn and climbed again in altitude. The pilot's voice crackled on the intercom announcing the weather was again too bad for a safe landing and he was turning back to Memphis.

Most passengers just shrugged their shoulders and shook their heads, but one question did remain. The pilot had mentioned refueling. Did that mean we were low on fuel?

Not long after that thought crossed my mind, the pilot announced we did have enough fuel and we shouldn't have any trouble landing. Smiles were exchanged with other passengers, and not too much later we landed safely.

I'm still not sure what was going on with the weather, the back and forth turns, or the pilot, but I knew I was safe with God. And yes, I'll admit it is much easier being brave when I'm filled with praise music.

I have no idea who piloted that plane, but I know who pilots my life. Even in the storms, the wild twists and turns, the days wondering if there will be enough fuel to make it through the day, we can rest assured a happy ending is coming.

As followers of Christ, we don't have to live in fear. We may live in a fallen world with falling bodies, but our inner soul is being renewed day by day. As Christians, we will live forever in the happily-ever-after. Our days are numbered in God's book. He knows the day we fly home, and no one or nothing can alter God's perfect plan. He knows the beginning and the end, and no one can snatch us from His hand. We are invincible in Christ.

Soooo as an invincible, shouldn't we be living an invincible life?

Do you realize what a difference that would make in our lives -- to know, truly know, we are invincible?

I thought about this fact when people were driving crazy around us on the interstate. I didn't have to worry because I'm invincible. Then when I pulled into a parking lot and a car full of men surveyed me in not-too-friendly terms. Not a problem, I'm invincible.

And the other night when I thought my brain had caught on fire and my head might explode. That was a problem, but I'm still invincible.

Would you live differently if you knew you had a 24/7 bodyguard? I would! I'd be fearless and super-brave.

For a few seasons a television show ran called Human Target. The information read: "It takes a brave, selfless man to make himself a 'human target' in order to save the lives of those in danger. For Chance, it's about one thing only: saving his clients' lives."

Interesting idea, and perhaps the premise sounds familiar? Christopher Chance was only a television character. Jesus Christ is real. When the punishment required for our sin meant death (being eternally separated from God), Jesus became the target in our place. When we choose to believe in Him, we are placed under His protection, and our souls are eternally safe.

In Christ, we have a 24/7 soul bodyguard. And who is bigger than God? What is bigger than God? What circumstance or situation is bigger than God? What person is bigger than God? What government is bigger than God? What past is too big for God? What present is too big for God? What future is too big for God?

Nothing and no one is bigger than our God.

We can trust God with our past, present, and future, because God is always in control, and in Christ we have an invincible eternity.

One evening we watched two videos made by a soft drink company with race driver, Jeff Gordon. Jeff, disguised as an older gentleman, visited a car dealership and took an unsuspecting car salesman on the test drive of his life.

The poor car salesman was terrified, horrified, and screamed during much of the wild, fast-speed "test" drive. By the time Jeff pulled back in the sales lot, the salesman jumped out of the car ready to call the police. However, when Jeff identified himself, the man's face showed relief, then delight. And he asked, "Want to do it again?"

Once the video went viral, several journalists claimed the video was a fake. So the soft drink company and Jeff again teamed up.

This time disguised as a cab driver, Jeff took one of the unsuspecting automotive journalists who had questioned the authenticity of the original "Test Drive" on a hair-raising, crazy ride. The man screamed, kicked, and begged to get out. However, when Jeff came to a stop and identified himself, the journalist wanted to go again.

The thing that struck me was, how many times people (even Christians) beg, scream, curse, and demand to get out of difficult situations even though God is in control. I understand because I want to bail out of bad situations. Life is hard, and pain is real. But what if we truly realized our loving God is always in control and instead we enjoyed the ride?

What if we remembered (never forgot) that God is with us, and His power, wisdom, and strength are in the driving seat?

What if we remembered the truth in God's word to, "Consider it pure joy, my brothers and sisters, whenever you face trials of many kinds, because you know that the testing of your faith produces perseverance. Let perseverance finish its work so that you may be mature and complete, not lacking anything." (James 1:2-4, NIV)

What if we remembered to be strong and courageous because God is with us wherever we go?[40]

What if we joyfully buckled in knowing that each trial, each wild ride, results in more strength, power, and knowledge that God is in control and our faith is growing stronger?

Let's trust God. Let's do it again! Buckle up. Your soul is always safe. You are invincible, and your loving Heavenly Father is in control.

God wants us to step into each new day with confidence. Often that means stepping outside of our comfort zones to reveal new and exciting adventures. When we step outside of our comfort zones we are able to see God working beyond them.

By stepping outside the problems of today and remembering to be grateful and praise God, we find our souls uplifted.

By living in God's Spirit, we keep in step with His Spirit. By keeping our feet on God's pathway, our steps remain sure. By stepping out of ourselves, we step closer to His presence.

Venturing outside of our boxed ideas, thoughts, and reasoning, we can watch how God works out of the box of our ideas, thoughts, and reasoning.

When I think I need to act in a certain way because I'm a Christian, I box myself into an imaginary box. My self-made box never fits because we aren't boxed-in or created to look like clones of one another, we are to allow Christ to mold us in His image.

Oh my goodness, I have confined myself for years worried about everything I say and do, and goodness knows makeup must be worn if stepping outside the door. I feel guilty if I don't have a quiet time, and then feel guilty if my quiet time isn't long enough or if I spend too much time doing one thing and not another thing. I'm boxed in until I can't move or breathe, and I've lost my joy. Gasp, wheeze...

Perhaps God just wants me to open my eyes and tell Him good morning. I think God wants us to crawl out of our self-made boxes or boxes that someone else has placed around us, and enjoy Him.

I'm the one who has made being a Christian SO hard. When I release all my worries about being "good" enough and acting "good" enough, I remember the simplicity of the life God has called us to live.

"...the Lord has told you what is good, and this is what he requires of you: to do what is right, to love mercy, and to walk humbly with your God" (Micah 6:8, NLT).

I can love God freely instead of thinking I need to do something to check off a mark on a list or please people. So, when the guilt thing is guilting me into feeling miserable, I need to remember condemnation doesn't come from God, in Christ we are free to be His unique creations, walking with Him, loving Him and loving others, unboxed to walk in the newness of Him.

Sometimes it's hard to get out of our boxes. Boxes can be kinda comfortable in an uncomfortable sort of way. To unbox ourselves takes trust to trust that God will protect our little unboxed selves.

I started wondering if I even really understood what trusting God really means. My simple mind needs simple explanations, so I used the Webster's 1828 Dictionary to find out more about the word "Trust." (The 1828 dictionary gives definitions and Bible verses. I love this resource, and it's online if you have a computer.)

I need help to understand things. I need to dig, analyze, and break things down to the basic levels, because my brain operates on pretty basic levels.

I'm going to share the definition, but would you do me a favor and really look at the definition to make it personal? Read slowly as you look at each word and see what stands out for you.

TRUST is confidence; a reliance or resting of the mind on the integrity, veracity, justice, friendship or other sound principle of another person. Something committed to a person's care for use or management, and for which an account must be rendered. Confidence; special reliance on supposed honesty. To place confidence in; to rely on, to believe; to credit, to commit to the care of, in confidence.

As I tried to understand what all of that meant, this verse came to mind, "Trust in the Lord with all your heart and lean not on your own understanding. In all your ways acknowledge Him, and He will direct your paths" (Proverbs 3:5-6, NASB).

The more we research and meditate on God's Word, the more we understand and the deeper the truth goes into our hearts, minds, and souls.

"Trust" according to Strong's H982 –is to trust, trust in, to have confidence, be confident, to be bold, to be secure, to cause to trust, make secure, to feel safe.

The more we dig into the Bible and find the deeper meanings, the more we can apply

God's truth to our lives. Another definition of "trust" is in Strong's H4009-- refuge, confidence, act of confiding, object of confidence, state of confidence, security.

So when we trust God, we remain in the state of confident trust because we know Who is our Trust.

Bold, courageous, resting in God trust comes from knowing Him and acknowledging Him in all things.

Trust comes from shining the light on any unrest with the knowledge of who God is with the knowledge and revelation of our great God. The God who created the universe. The God who can do all things. The God of everything and everyone. The God who is not bound by space or time. The God who loves with an unfailing love. The God who will direct our paths, no matter where the journey, direction, or road leads.

Trust comes from remembering God, remembering His promises, remembering His provision, remembering (causing to know) God.

To know God is to trust Him! To Trust God is to know Him. To know Him is to TRUST HIM. The circular truth circles back again!

I've been under intense spiritual

warfare, and at times the sensations and emotions seemed overwhelming and hopeless. One night I dreamed I was in an oppressive darkness with the enemy closing in and I was surrounded. With human vision, no escape was possible.

And yet when I spoke the words, "I trust God!" I saw a visual of the rocky ground where I stood shoot up from the earth far above my enemies.

And I realized trusting God is the propellant.

Trusting God is rocket fuel that propels us skyward above our enemies.

Trusting God is the key.

Trusting God releases God's blessings.

Trusting God shoots us skyward to see more clearly our situation.

Trusting God releases the power of God to rocket us above the past, present, and future.

When we are engaged in battle with the enemy, we must know what is truly written in God's word.

The devil twists the truth. Therefore, we need to know The Truth. When Jesus was tempted by Satan He quoted scripture by saying, "It is written" (see Matthew 4:1-11).

Every one of us will undergo temptations; enemy attacks with doubts, fears, questions, and condemnation. Satan is a liar, and he twists the truth. God's word is truth, and we must know God's word which is ***The Truth***. Jesus said, "If you continue in My word, then you are truly disciples of Mine; and you will know the truth, and the truth will make you free" (John 8:31-32, NASB).

When the tempter comes, quote God's word, know what is written in the Bible, for in God's word the truth sets you free.

And when Satan gives you a hard time, remember You are from God and have overcome the enemy because God is greater in you than Satan who is in the world (1 John 4:4).

Our enemy is defeated, and you are an overcomer because of the blood of the Lamb and because of the word of your testimony (Revelation 12:11).

So remember...

> "...no weapon turned against you will succeed. You will silence every voice raised up to accuse you. These benefits are enjoyed by the

> servants of the Lord; their vindication will come from me. I, the Lord, have spoken!" (Isaiah 54:17, NLT).
>
> "The Lord is a shelter for the oppressed, a refuge in times of trouble" (Psalm 9:9, NLT).
>
> "I know the Lord is always with me. I will not be shaken, for he is right beside me" (Psalm 16:8, NLT).
>
> "The Lord is my rock, my fortress, and my savior; my God is my rock, in whom I find protection. He is my shield, the power that saves me, and my place of safety" (Psalm 18:2, NLT).

Search God's word, find what is written, for the written word saves, the written word protects, the written word is freedom.

If bad days or bad dreams hit and leave you reeling, remember God's truth.

Two o'clock in the morning and my eyes flew open. Another bad dream. I was sick at the time, and already worried about getting older, weaker, and being alone.

In the darkness, I whispered the name – *Jesus* — The Name of my Savior and rescuer. I prayed for help.

And verses came with reminders that God will never leave or forsake us.[41]

That God is with us even when we get old.[42]

That God will be with us through the hard things and the fires of life.[43]

That God is always faithful and His mercies are new every morning.[44]

That God is our strength.[45]

That God cares for us and won't let the righteous fall.[46]

That God will meet all our needs.[47]

When you are afraid and worried, wrap up those worries in God's truth and smother those fears and worries away.

Another night I woke worried about an extended family member. (Do you notice how the enemy strikes in the darkness? Ack!)

Flopping, tossing, and turning I wrestled with my concerns and hoped God was listening.

Then it hit me, I needed to remember to praise. Philippians 4:6-7 tells us "Don't worry about anything; instead, pray about everything. Tell God what you need, and thank him for all he has done. Then you will experience God's peace, which exceeds anything we can understand. His peace will guard your hearts and minds as you live in Christ Jesus."[48]

I definitely needed peace, so I flipped my concerns into praises.

The prayers went from, "Help _ _ _ _ _ _ with their situation" to "Thank You Father that no situation is too big for You."

Every concern was turned to a praise. As the focus changed, the prayers became bigger, and the strength became bigger, and the comfort became bigger, and the peace became bigger, and the knowledge of God's might and power, became **bigger**.

The problems that loomed so very large at the beginning became tiny in the presence of Almighty, loving, all-magnificent, creator of the universe, nothing-is-impossible God.

Whatever is bothering you, whatever is gnawing at your soul, refocus the focus by flipping the requests into praises and watch as God soothes your soul.

Over and over God has revealed the importance of praise.

I've been in a situation that left me worried and confused. I couldn't see clearly, couldn't even think of how to pray about the issue, so I decided to sing praise songs and get my mind off my problems and back on God.

Then the coolest thing happened. As I sang praise songs and praised God, the confusion lifted, and I was given clarity. Peace and answers came and joy followed. So I praised all the more, and God showed me His truth, and the confusion ended, and peace, joy, and clarity returned.[49]

Praise is like a mind windshield wiper. Praise wipes away confusion to see things clearly through God's perspective.

When the brain is muddied and confused with worries, and you can't see what to do or where to go, activate praising God for clarity, peace, and joy. If we don't remember what God has done and thank God, our thinking gets more foolish and our hearts are darkened. Romans 12:1 warns, "Don't let your thinking be futile and don't be foolish. For although they knew God, they neither glorified him as God nor gave thanks to him, but their thinking became futile and their foolish hearts were darkened" (Romans 1:21, NIV).

I don't know about you, but the last thing I want is a dark, foolish heart.

Let me share another truth about praise.

Wesley Duewel said praise is a Christian's spiritual heavy artillery and more effective than an atom bomb in battle.[50]

The last thing Satan wants you to do is praise God, so praise and let the spiritual bombs fly.

The enemy wants you to think the situation is impossible -- instead remember with God all things are possible and praise God.

The enemy wants you to think you've been defeated -- instead remember the devil has already been defeated and praise God for His victory.

The enemy wants you to do nothing but whine and stay in the dark -- instead praise God and let His light shine through you.

The enemy wants you to give up -- instead look up and praise God.

When we come to God in praise and thanksgiving, we aren't ignoring our problems, heartaches, or concerns. In praise and thanksgiving, we are brought into God's presence where we can remember the might, power, and majesty of our awesome God.

Praise and thanksgiving puts everything back into proper perspective giving us vision beyond what our earthly eyes can see.

Without corrective lenses, my vision is terribly flawed. Fortunately, the doctor helps with a proper prescription. I can't just buy a pair of glasses off the rack, can't borrow a friend's reading glasses, or even use ones I've had in the past. My eyes need to be given the proper lenses for the proper vision.

In the same way, we have to make sure we see through God's truth. There are those who say, "This is how I see, so you also should see my way." Even the media has power for good or evil based on how they report. The angle of the camera can be used to sway public opinion.

Editors can edit video and audio to present what they want you to see and hear. People can do the same by only giving information to help their cause or further their agenda. Churches, friendships, families, and countries have split from inaccurate vision.

Society, culture, the latest fads, the latest popular sin of the day tries to rewrite and alter God's truth to fit their desires. God has to be first. His truth has to be first, and His truth doesn't change with the times. God's truth is timeless because He is timeless.

God's truth exposes any entrenched lies in our thinking.

I kept getting stuck in my writing, and I asked God to expose anything hindering my creativity. Then I remembered a comment from someone I had known. Stuck back in the recesses of my mind a statement that lady had made had wedged in my thoughts like a doubt roadblock.

God's truth exposed the lie reminding me that ALL things are possible for God. What is impossible for men is not impossible for God, because nothing is impossible for God.

In my own limited understanding I was merely stumbling in the dark groping for a solution. Yet when I ran to God's light, His truth exposed the lie.

Jesus is the light, the truth, and the Word which brings wisdom. When we turn to the light of Christ and ask for His wisdom, His truth will expose any hindrance.

Another tactic by the enemy to not get us to trust God is to bug us with the worry bug.

Jesus repeatedly tells us to not worry. He's got us covered every moment of every day. Every minute I've spent in worry, I'm telling God I don't trust in His power and guidance. The more I worry, the more I have pulled away from His presence. Worry indicates a lack of faith in God to handle the situation, and a lack of belief that He loves me enough to care for me.

As I wrestled with worries, I came up with some questions to help me get my perspective back on track.

Will my worrying actually help anything or anyone?

Does worrying about what someone else thinks of me actually change how they think of me, or how they think?

Does worrying about what someone else has done actually change what they've done?

Does my worrying show my faith in God?

Does my worrying remember that nothing is impossible for God?

Does my worrying help my mind, body, heart, and soul?

Does my worrying show that I love God with all my heart, mind, body, and soul?

Is worrying worth my time?

Is worrying worth my health?

Is the act of worrying positive in any way?

The answer to all the questions is ...

NO!!!!!

So how can I stop the worry process? By taking thoughts captive and replace the worries with God's truth and love.

I changed my questions to statements.

My faith in God's truth and love will actually help anything and/or anyone.

My faith in God's truth and love will help me focus beyond what someone else thinks of me and may actually change how they think of me and others.

My faith in God's truth and love will help me stop worrying about what someone else has done.

My faith in God's truth and love will show my faith in God.

My faith in God's truth and love will help me remember that nothing is impossible for God.

My faith in God's truth and love will help my mind, body, heart, and soul.

My faith in God's truth and love will show that I love God with all my heart, mind, body, and soul.

My faith in God's truth and love will is worth all my time.

My faith in God's truth and love is positive for my health.

My faith in God's truth and love will is

positive in every way!

Remember Worry is just a

Wicked
Onslaughting
Runaway
Rowdy
Yowl

Take thoughts captive and banish those wicked, onslaughting, runaway, rowdy, yowling worries with God's truth and love.

The closer we are to God and the more we meditate on His truth and love, the less we look over our shoulders at the past or worry about the future.

God is the God of the past, present, and future. He knows every need and every situation. God is trustworthy. No matter where life may lead you, you can trust God every moment of every day. When troubles and worries come calling, call upon the Lord.

There is nothing (no situation, no person, and no event) too big for God. The maker of the universe, the One who holds the world in His hands and your soul in His protection will overcome any obstacle to fly you safely home.

Flying Through the Battle While Battling Through the Flight

The smell of rank cigarette smoke filled the jetliner. Praying desperately not to lose the contents of my stomach, I hunched over in my seat. I had flown to Canada on business and was now returning home. The airlines had not yet banned smoking on flights and whatever filled the compartment had made me horribly nauseous. That was one of my worst flights ever.

I've experienced hair-raising experiences while traveling. During an early-morning flight, the jet's landing gear wouldn't lock in place. Our plane circled to burn off fuel as firetrucks, ambulances, and emergency vehicles lined the runway.

The jet was filled with business people like myself. No one panicked as the pilot briefed us on the difficulties. A few passengers did press their call buttons and ask the stewardess for a drink, making mention they could at least medicate us before we hit the ground.

Fortunately, the pilot managed to keep the nose of the jet pointed upward until the final landing jolt popped the gear back into a locked position, and we landed without incident.

I think most people who travel have had some kind of interesting experience -- whether baggage was lost or misrouted, a bumpy flight, or an annoying seatmate. There's always something that can make traveling a challenge.

Some days I don't even have to leave the house to find challenging situations. For months I found myself in a major spiritual battle. HORRIBLE. Worst ever. Most discouraging. WORST EVER! Did I mention it was bad?

Life with my husband and son was great, but my internal spiritual battle was AWFUL. Did I mention it was really bad?

All I wanted was for the battle to end, to find the safe place in God's heart and crawl away from the troubles of the world, but I couldn't find God's heart.

I couldn't even find God.

I tried to crawl off the battlefield and the howl that scratched at my soul, and I couldn't seem to get away. Trying to drown the screams from within, I busied myself and still couldn't find peace. I worked in the house, cleaned, ran errands, and worked in the yard. Still the soul-isolation shredded from inside out, and I felt my heart tearing into a million pieces. I begged God to show me where I had gone wrong, yet heaven stayed silent.

I begged God not to waste whatever caused this pain, that somehow He would be glorified, yet heaven stayed silent.

I so wanted to reach out for help from friends, but everyone seemed to be fighting their own raging battles. The wounds kept bleeding, the heart continued fainting, and heaven stayed silent. I begged to die, and heaven stayed silent.

Perhaps you've been there, been at the place where heaven seemed silent and distant. Perhaps you are there now in the midst of a battle.

This world is full of trouble, and sometimes that trouble is too much to bear. With no end in sight and in the midst of the sightless mess you can't see God.

I wish I could tell you I found that perfect button to push, the one that makes God appear and all trouble flee. I haven't.

There are times my troubles rolled away in a flash as I read the Bible, prayed, sang praise songs, and heaven responded.

But there are times NOTHING seems to help. There are times the enemy seems stronger, faster, and more diabolical than the goodness of God can fight.

(Illness, bodies and brains running amuck can add to the battle and at those times doctors and counselors are life-savers. Please don't ignore seeking medical help when needed.)

When problems are coming from something other than health-related issues. When nothing seems to work. When life is a roller coaster ride with hair-raising drops and upside-down turns and even the barf-bags can't be found, those are the times that it's a battle of the will—a battle to will yourself to remember how battles are won.

It's willing ourselves to remember the truth of who we are in Christ and that we are eternally safe and invincible in Christ.

It's willing ourselves to remember God promised to fight for us. He promised to never leave us or forsake us. He promised

His love is unfailing.

It's willing ourselves to remember battles aren't won by caving to the enemy. Battles are won by remembering as a Christian we are on the winning team.

It's willing ourselves to remember crawling off the battlefield isn't an option because until the end a battle will always rage. It's willing ourselves to remember the enemy may battle, but the final war has already been won.

It's willing ourselves to remember we are to run into the battles where God calls us because no battle is too big for our God.

Satan wants us to withdraw, to put down our swords, to curl into a ball, and have nothing to do with anyone or with God.

The enemy wants to silence you, get you off the battlefield so your testimony can't help and encourage others. Your life is here to point others to The Life, so don't believe for a moment you don't have a purpose.

Wherever you are in the battle, remember you are never alone. Watch for how God is working, how God is using you, and has positioned you to help others.

Let's keep the enemy from winning any more ground! Let's stop believing the lie we should crawl off the battlefield.

Beyond human sight, the battles rage between the forces of good and evil. The enemy is slinking around, sliming his slime in our thoughts and trying every dirty trick to keep people away from the love of God.

Satan wants Christians to be ineffective or throw in the towel. Our hearts are under attack because the enemy wants our hearts to stop beating passionately for Christ. Don't let the enemy win! Put up heart guards by listening to God's word and keeping the wisdom learned in God's truth.[51]

If you feel surrounded by the enemy, don't worry, that only makes them easier to hit.

When fear attacks, attack fear with God's truth and watch fear turn tail and run. The Bible is an offensive weapon against the enemy providing the sword of truth, and that sword slashes away every attack of the enemy. Read God's word, say the words, go to God with every request because God is more than a safe place to run, God is our defender and protector. He is our shield.[52]

Psalm 91 has been one of my favorite refuge chapters, a place to read and hide in the shadow of God's wings, curled up safe and out of the battle. The other day in the midst of a spiritual battle I realized Psalm 91 as much more – the words are a fortress of safety in the heat of war, the invincibility of those who abide in God's presence. God offers life delivered not from trouble but life delivered in the midst of trouble.

God's word is alive and active. As you dig, you find more treasure. As your life moves forward, His Word continues to flow into your ever-flowing life. Jesus is the living water. He is The Life, The Way, and The Truth that shows you the way to truly live life.

Stand firm. Put on your armor. Grab your sword of the spirit, fight, and allow God to fight for you. Rely on God's power and might. And His life will again breathe life.

"In the event of an emergency decompression, an oxygen mask will automatically appear in front of you." If you've flown on an airliner, the pre-flight announcements usually include that statement.

I have a paper bag with the word "faith" written on the side. I originally made the bag to share at a speaking engagement, but I keep it with me for those really tough days. I need my faith paper bag when I need my faith not to hyper-ventilate because there are days the battle is overwhelming. I pick up the faith bag and breathe again.

It takes faith to make it through the days, faith to make it through the long nights, and faith to take a step or lay in bed when you are too ill to move.

Maybe the word "faith" seems too big, too daunting, too much in the midst of trials and difficulties.

I checked the original Greek definition of the word "faith." According to Strongs G4102[53]. Generally speaking, faith is the conviction that God exists and is the creator and ruler of all things, a belief that Jesus is the Messiah, a trust and confidence in God and Jesus.

I realized even when I think my faith is small, I have faith in God and Jesus.

Maybe when I'm not living in victorious faith is when I think my faith has to be in what *I* can accomplish as a Christian. I need to remember I can do all things **through Christ** who strengthens me. Faith comes by trusting Christ, not trusting me. Even tiny faith can move mountains.

Warriors are needed. Overcomers. Those who will trust God even in the midst of the bloody battles. We need those who will strap on the faith bag and keep moving forward. We need those who will share their faith bag with those who can't breathe.

Those titles – warrior, overcomer – aren't only for super-heroes and legends. Every breath you take is proof you are a warrior and overcomer. Every breath you take is proof that God is breathing faith into your soul.

Revelation 12:11 speaks of those who overcame the enemy by the blood of the Lamb and the word of their testimony. Overcoming is in our DNA as Christians. Through Christ's sacrifice we are given the right to overcome. Through our words and stories, we can show others how God moved, guided, healed, renewed, and carried us through to overcome.

I'll be honest, the last thing I feel like right now is a warrior. I'm sitting here on the verge of tears wondering why on earth I'm writing. I've battled through hardships, trials, illness, and major messes, but writing has taken a toll. I hold out my heart to people through writing and there are days no one seems to notice. The comments don't come, not even a little thumbs up on Facebook. And I wonder why should I even bother?

I'm going to lay it all out because only

God knows if someone will read this. God has blessed amazingly in my life even with all the hardships, but I've really been wimpy and whining.

It's too easy to compare success based on what I think other writers, bloggers, or ministry friends have accomplished. I watch their pages and notice their books in the bookstores and wonder why I seem to live in the shadows. My biggest warrior battles are often with myself. Human nature is so blasted human. I want to see beyond an earthly perspective. I SO want to see life from God's perspective, to see beyond basing success on numbers, or who notices whom, and who gets more comments.

I want dots to connect in ways I think they should connect. But that's like picking up a paint-by-number set, and instead of painting, I connect dots, then complain the picture doesn't look right and isn't as pretty as I imagined.

My earthly perspective is flawed. I notice those who are "successful" with mega-followers and books printed by major publishers, and I wonder if I'm missing God's mark. So I try to do what other's do, try to market in ways other authors market, and nothing works in the ways I think they will work.

My writing hasn't been the only thing that tripped me up. When I worked in business, I compared myself to other workers. When our son was young, I'd compare myself to other mothers. As a woman, I compare myself to other women. On and on, and on and on, the comparisons keep comparing until my head spins off my neck, and I'm left in a crying heap on the floor.

In that mess of comparing, I find I'm trying do everything in my own strength, using my small brain and my finite understanding instead of resting in God and following His leading by remembering He made me and loves me for me.

If I only notice how I think others are blessed, I will miss out on seeing how I am blessed.

When comparing, when I wish there were more and want earthly success, I don't notice the blessings of what God has done and is doing in my writing and my own life.

When will I learn earthly dots are flawed dots? They are inaccurate and will never connect how God is working in the eternal heavenlies.

If you think you are laboring away and

no one notices, please remember God notices you. He sees your work. He knows you are up late at night taking care of your family. He knows the difficulties at your job and at home. He understands, and He is blessing you in heavenly ways you might not see at this moment.

God always blesses His faithful servants. So keep at it, friend. Keep running your race and doing what God has called you to do because it will be worth it all when you step into heaven.

Writing this book has been a battle. I've stopped and started, stopped and started. I'd move forward. Then doubts and fears would creep in, and I'd pull away. I'd get excited and enthused and return to write. Then I'd be sobbing at my inadequacies and wondering who on earth will want to read another book by Lisa Buffaloe? Seriously? Me?

I realized this book doesn't have the answers you seek but can point to the Bible which has every answer for every problem. I'm not a savior, but I can point to The Savior. It's not what I can do, but how can I serve my Savior. It's not about making money, but making disciples for Christ.

The lie is that I have to be perfect to

point to a perfect Savior. It's a lie! Jesus came to the messy and the outcast. God chose the little guys to take on the big guys. He chooses the weak to be strong and the simple ones to confound the wise.

I'm going to preach to myself -- stop trying to be perfect. Jesus is the only perfect one, so point to Him and live your life as He said to live -- loving God and loving people.

I'm not the perfect writer, but somehow God will use my writing (if I will write through Him) to touch lives. I can think of so many people whose lives touched mine by their words – family members, friends, pastors, teachers, authors, and even strangers helped me along my pathway by their words.

Your words matter. Your words make a difference. Whatever you feel led to do, whatever you are called to do, do it for God. Work for Him. Not people. Not to make a name for yourself. Not to be successful in the world's eyes. Love God and let His love pop out of you in whatever you do.

A friend reminded me the other day of Paul's ministry. It's easy to read the Bible and see all his letters and his great faith and think, "Wow, this guy did it all!" However, if you look at his ministry, everything looked like a failure.

Read Paul's own account of his journey in 2 Corinthians 11:25--- "Three times I was beaten with rods, once I was pelted with stones, three times I was shipwrecked, I spent a night and a day in the open sea, I have been constantly on the move. I have been in danger from rivers, in danger from bandits, in danger from my fellow Jews, in danger from Gentiles; in danger in the city, in danger in the country, in danger at sea; and in danger from false believers. I have labored and toiled and have often gone without sleep; I have known hunger and thirst and have often gone without food; I have been cold and naked." (NIV)

Now does that sound successful? From an earthly perspective Paul was anything but effective. Ah but that heavenly perspective reveals he truly had an amazingly successful ministry.

We are all called to love God and love people. Loving can come with our words and our actions. God's heavenly perspective is beyond what we can grasp with our own vision.

I want to see like Elisha's servant and see the heavenly army's protection even when the enemy is overwhelming (see 2

Kings 6:10-17). Elisha prayed for his servant's eyes to be opened. "Then the Lord opened the servant's eyes, and he looked and saw the hills full of horses and chariots of fire all around Elisha."[54] Woot! I love that!

Oh, if we could only see God's armies at work. God does more than we can think or imagine. Elisha saw. He knew the heavenly army was there.

I think there is so much more waiting to experience and be seen than we can even fathom. There is a reality of heavenly steps that connect the dots that one day will explain everything. One day we will truly understand what happened and why things happened, and all the suffering and mess of this world will be washed away, healed, restored, and made new.

For every action there is a reaction. So if I act in faith, will my faith react? If I act in belief, will my belief react?

Ah! There's the key!

When I act by standing on God's truth, truly God's truth will help me stand.

When I activate my faith, my faith will reactivate.

When I act in belief, my belief will react.

In Matthew 5, Jesus shows the blessed

reaction of actions. For those who are poor in spirit, they receive the kingdom. For those who are mourn, they will be comforted. The meek inherit the earth. Those who are hungering and thirsting for righteousness will be filled. The merciful receive mercy. The pure in heart see God. The peacemakers are called the children of God. Those who are persecuted receive God's kingdom and an eternal reward. For every action there is a reaction.

Over five years ago I purchased a print to hang over our fireplace. I bought the painting because it reminded me of a scene I had "seen."

My best friend/sister-in-law Kathy had died, and God blessed with a dream (or vision) of seeing her in heaven. In the distance I could see hills/mountains with Italian looking villas. My earthly vision was clouded, but the scene brought hope for the future and comfort for my grieving heart.

The picture hung over our fireplace in the family room, and I'd look up and wonder and try to see that scene again of the heavenly hope.

We've now moved to Tennessee, and the print is leaning against the wall in my office waiting again to be hung. As I look I see something I don't remember noticing -- a group of villas in the distance. I could claim this new discovery is because of a new angle or the lighting, but in reality I think it's because I've been looking, straining, to recreate my dream.

Y'all for OVER five years, I missed reality. Now don't get me wrong, I believe I saw Kathy in heaven. I believe God gave me a glimpse of the heavenly beauty to come, but I missed the beauty of a painting I've had for **years** because I wanted to see something else.

I've decided earthly dots are mainly what we imagine based on earth-based logic. Since we can't see the future, our brains take off and run in a direction trying to fill in the dots. Earthly dot connection often imagines the worst-case scenario.

Examples...

1. A friend doesn't return email. Brain goes crazy trying to analyze and wonders if the friendship is over, and wonders does the friend care anymore, and what was said or done to offend?

Reality ... friend's email is down, or friend is going through difficulties and doesn't want to discourage and plans on emailing soon, or a myriad of non-earth-shattering issues.

2. A three-year-old has a meltdown, and the imagination goes wild for the mom. Earthly dots connect to worry that she's the worst-mom-ever, child will have anger issues, probably need incarceration, and mom will never win the best mom award.

Reality ... child is tired and needs a nap. Mom is doing great to manage whining toddler. Both will survive and do just fine. (Even if your kid is a mess, there are many amazing adults who started out as messy kids. Actually, I think most of us were pretty messy kids. So young moms, please don't give up hope, relax and enjoy your messy child.)

We can also inaccurately connect dots because we see what we want to see. Such as, he/she wants the best for me because they said so, but remember to look at how they treat you, not just what they say. Look at the fruit! We are told to be wise as serpents gentle as doves. If someone is abusive, seek help and get out of that relationship.

We need to connect the right dots.

Heavenly dots don't look at what's missing. They can "see" what is true, noble, right, pure, lovely, admirable, excellent, and praiseworthy. The Bible is a light to our feet and a lamp to our path bringing vision to know where, and how, to stand.

Heavenly dots are seen through praise and gratitude. An amazing truth and blessing is that we enter the courts of God through praise and thanksgiving.[55] Think about that for a minute; we can enter the courts of God. Wow! What an honor and privilege!

A heavenly mindset is available for Christians because we are seated in the heavenlies. When we become Christians we are given the right, and the blessing of being able to see through heavenly vision. Maybe we don't see because we don't ask to see. James tells us we don't have because we don't ask or we ask with the wrong motives (James 4:2-3).

I wonder how many times I've tried to analyze a situation or person, sit and stew about a situation or person, worry about a situation or person, plot and plan about a situation or person, instead of asking God for discernment, wisdom, and help. Goodness, it's like I'm walking around without my glasses on (and without glasses I'm an accident waiting to happen).

We are in a battle, but we aren't left defenseless, and we aren't left without a proper perspective. It's up to us to ask for God's help, to read the Bible so we have holy ammunition ready and our faith shields activated.

The enemy is always taking shots at us, trying to shoot us down, keep us down and grounded in earthly issues and problems. The last thing Satan wants is a victorious Christian flying through the battles of life.

I've taken hits, lots of hits on my little wings, and some days I feel like a World War II flying ace. My little Buffaloe wings are tattered and pock-marked, but they are also marked by moments of victories.

Thankfully, no matter how battered or beaten our wings, God teaches us to fly. Flight training involves well … training. God's flight school reveals how to fly even when engines are on fire and the fuselage is ripped open with hundreds of bullet holes.

In the Bible we are given examples of those who have seen beyond the fog of life and seen beyond the ordinary.

I'm always amazed a pilot can land an airplane without a visual of the ground. In the middle of darkness, storms, or fog, how do they see? I know they have instrumentation and radar, but it's still pretty incredible.

During winter months, Boise, Idaho, could be trapped in an inversion. Warm air rises, and the cold air settles in the valley. The clouds settle in a foggy soup. It's cold, and the more the pollution builds, the heavier and more toxic the air.

Yet by if we drive up the mountain, the air is clear, warmer, and the sun is shining. In the same way, if we don't rise up and keep our focus on Jesus, The Son, we risk our minds being fogged by the toxicity of the world, our past, and the difficulties of life.

The Son is always shining, always ready to burn away the fog of discouragement, disillusionment, and despair. But we have to be looking, watching, and expecting something different than what the world has to offer.

Beyond the ordinary fog of life there are extraordinary things happening.

Two thousand years ago the heavens had been silent for so very long. Then an ordinary young virgin and an ordinary carpenter were chosen to be part of a very extraordinary event.

Extraordinary life took on ordinary skin, and a tiny baby squirmed and cried in the midst of a dirty stable. Jesus Christ, born in Bethlehem with no fanfare, no paparazzi, no entourage, no castle for a King, nothing extraordinary to be noticed by man.

Ordinary shepherds watching their sheep heard the message of an extraordinary event, and they ran to worship.

Eight days after his birth, Jesus was taken to the temple by Joseph and Mary to present an offering to God. They only had a very poor offering, for they were very poor, just an ordinary couple. Yet an elderly man, Simeon, saw beyond the ordinary because he had been looking for God's fulfillment of extraordinary love through the Messiah.

Anna, a very old woman who never left the temple, watched, prayed and waited. She saw an ordinary baby who was the extraordinary Messiah, and she rejoiced.[56]

The Magi from the east watched and followed an extraordinary star, traveling far to find a king in ordinary flesh, and they worshiped.

Simeon and Anna, the Magi, the shepherds, saw Jesus. They saw through the ordinary. Truth is revealed to those who watch and seek. Truth comes through the Holy Spirit who testifies and reveals beyond what mortal eyes can see.

You too can see beyond the ordinary. Jesus is the truth, the life, and the light. His grace gifts us to live far from ordinary lives because our hearts carry an extraordinary Savior.

We don't have to miss how God is working. We don't have to be limited by earthly vision or human logic. Every moment of every day God is working in extraordinary ways. Be one who watches, seeks, and sees beyond the ordinary to notice the glory of an extraordinary God. Let's ask for a beyond ordinary mindset to set our minds on the extraordinary heavenly perspective.

One evening Jesus sent his disciples ahead to cross the lake. Then a storm hit.[57] Most of the guys were fishermen who understood storms and how to pilot a boat. This wasn't just a rain shower, this was a big storm, a massive one that scared them to death.

Scholars estimate the disciples struggled for close to nine hours. Their boat was pounded by wind and rain and battered by waves. Every muscle in their bodies taxed to the limit as they struggled, rowed, and prayed for help.

As the storm raged, Jesus came to them,[58] "Don't be afraid. Take courage. I'm here."[59]

Jesus came for His disciples, and He will come for you. Even though the wait is so very long. Whatever your situation, no matter how high the waves, or how strong the winds, don't be afraid. Take courage. He is with you to rescue and save. He will be with you and will never fail or abandon you.[60] No storm is too big; no waves are too wild for Jesus to save.

Don't give up. Don't give in to the enemy's lies that you are alone.

Although I have a wonderful family and sweet friends, there are times I'm lonely. Not just a passing loneliness but a desperate, aching soul-cry loneliness.

I want to go home, really go home to my heavenly home, because God is The One who knows me inside and out, who is never too tired or too busy to listen, who is never too preoccupied with life that He won't live life with me. There are times I SO long for someone who will help me process through the process of living on this messed-up earth.

I'm not alone in these feelings of loneliness. Even David cried out to God, "Turn to me and be gracious to me, for I am lonely and afflicted" (Psalm 25:16, NASB).

Perhaps you too are struggling. The enemy wants you to believe you are all alone, that nobody understands, nobody loves you, and nobody really wants to hear what's on your heart.

The truth is, God understands, God loves you, and He always wants to hear what's on your heart.

When loneliness seeks to depress, press into God. In the loneliness, seek Him – seek His face, seek His heart, and seek His word. Lonely one, your heart is always at home in God's heart. His word promises, "God makes a home for the lonely..." (Psalm 68:6, NASB).

In 1947, pilot Chuck Yeager broke the sound barrier. He reported the turbulence was terrible right before he broke through, but after the breakthrough the air was as smooth as glass.

I wonder how often in the midst of

major turmoil and difficulties we are actually on the brink of a breakthrough. Satan wants to stop us in any way possible. Yet if we keep moving forward with God's help, we can break through any barrier.

Remember, always remember, God's love is unfailing, His might and power are inexhaustible, and the evil forces of this world will fall. God ALWAYS Triumphs!

Keep flying through the battle and keep battling. With God's help, your breakthrough will breakthrough.

Catching Air Currents

High in the sky, the bird soared and danced in the wind. I longed to experience effortless flight. Then I realized the bird didn't study charts on air currents, he just flew on available winds.

We aren't birds, but we are given more than a puff of air every now and then. God gifts us with heavenly jet streams above the gale force winds of hardships and the boring daily tasks.

If we could grasp how great God's love is for us, I think we would be flying, unlimited, unbound, and free. Love gives power to fly. We don't have to wait for a special person to come into our life. God's love is available 24/7 for **every single one of us.**

God's love is deeper, richer, and wider than we can imagine. Even when the air currents of life are bumpy, stormy, and messy, we can stay airborne in the knowledge we are loved and kept by a Heavenly Father.

Jesus loves you, and His love is proof that someone loves you enough to die for you. His love is mercy that came before you ever needed His mercy.

At a speaking event for young moms, I asked those in attendance if they would sing the song, "Jesus Loves Me." Most in the audience quickly sang without hesitation.

I then asked them to sing making the song personal, to truly grasp they were loved by Jesus. The group was silent for a moment, then their words came out haltingly almost as though they couldn't believe it was true for themselves.

Do you know you are loved by God, that Jesus truly loves you?

If you hesitated, I understand. I've had many, many, many times I thought God couldn't love me. I didn't think I deserved His love because of some of the things I've done or thought. I deserve to be burnt toast, punished, cast aside, and cast out, but God still loved and still loves. And, God still loves you regardless of what you've done.

I mentioned earlier that God gives second chances. God's love never fails even when we fail. So would you take a moment to say the words, "God loves me. Jesus loves me."

Now point to your chest and say it again, "God loves me. Jesus loves me."

Regardless of how you are feeling and regardless of your circumstances, please smile and say again, "God loves me. Jesus loves me."

God's love is perfect love, love that is beyond the most gentle touch, the sweetest kiss, and the warmest embrace. Look at the magnificent mountains, the beauty of the sunset and sunrise, the sands on the beach, the blue of the ocean, and you have only glimpsed part of His love.

Take the most tender love ever known and multiply it by infinity and perhaps, just perhaps, you will begin to understand the love of God.

No matter how rich the human love, nothing and no one will love us as much, and no one can show us more that we are loved than God. God's love is faithful, compassionate, gracious, magnificent, infinite, overflowing, unfailing, and indefinable.

To be honest, it's difficult to find adequate descriptions of God's love --

amazing, wonderful, all fulfilling, all filling, forever hope, forever love, the love that is beyond anything this world can offer. I could fill the pages with descriptions but never come close to a complete portrayal of His love.

The truth is God loves you and Jesus loves you. You are loved. Don't allow the enemy, you, or anyone else to block you from flying free in the realization you are loved. As you allow God's truth to go soul deep, your wings are gonna sprout because you are speaking truth over your body, mind, and soul.

The other day I searched through radio stations trying to find a song as I drove home. I stopped when I heard a man's voice pleading with the one he loved not to leave him. His voice carried such emotion and angst I found my heart breaking.

A well of emotion split me open as I realized God made emotions. His heart must cry and bleed when we turn away or when we don't believe the depth of His love. I can't imagine the heart break of The One who made our hearts.

The Bible shows the relentless loving pursuit God has for people. He pleads. He stretches out His hands. He blesses and gives and loves, and yet so few will listen or respond.

God's love doesn't wane or ebb and flow based on what kind of day you've had or how you feel, or what you've done or haven't done. God's love is unfailing.

God's love is soul-food to every molecule of your being. When you say the words, "God loves me; Jesus loves me," you are infusing living water and the Bread of Life to water and feed your soul.

Our souls are made to love God, and when we love God, we connect with His perfect love. Again the circular truth comes: this amazing love given by God returns as we love Him. When we love the Lord with all our hearts, we have found a love which will never fail our hearts.

God's love is not ordinary love. God's love is power to love beyond our own capacities. Human love is never perfect love. Love the world, and the world often takes that love and squashes and squishes said love flat.

Years ago, I was contacted by someone online. Over a period of months, the friendship grew and the trust level grew. Then some difficult things started happening in my friend's life. I agonized, prayed, and counseled. I stayed up late into the night emailing and messaging through social interactions and helping in any way I could.

Then that person's story started unraveling. I realized most (if not all) of what they had shared was a lie. I had been sucked into a big fat lie, and my heart broke. I grieved. I felt the fool and wanted to stop caring, stop opening myself up to others, and pull away from people.

Fortunately, a Godly friend helped by reminding me I had responded in love by loving with God's love. I could continue to hold my head high. I could trust that whatever was going on God knew the truth.

Did it hurt? Yes. Heart hurts do hurt. And people can hurt us so very deeply.

I've been through other heart hurts too deep to even mention. Yet there is safety within God's love. He loves deep, wide, long, high, unhindered, and unfailing. God's love never pretends to be anything but the perfect love of a perfect God.

As we press into God's heart, we can love with His love. By loving with Gods love, His love fills with His unlimited love to love without limits.

When our hearts are placed in The

Hands that made our hearts, our heart is always safe and forever loved.

A heart that beats tender in the safety of God's love can bleed love eternal.

Jesus said, "Love the Lord your God with all your heart, with all your soul, and with all your mind.' This is the first and great commandment. And the second is like it: 'You shall love your neighbor as yourself" (Matthew 22:36-40, NKJV).

When Jesus tells us to love God, He is offering freedom because when we love the Lord with all our heart, soul, mind, and strength, everything aligns. Life makes sense because true life is found in The One who brings life.

Love the Lord your God with all your heart, and your heart finds home, comfort, and love.

Love the Lord your God with all your mind, and bad thoughts are taken captive; your mind becomes focused, single-minded on God in the peace of God.

Love the Lord your God with all your soul, and your soul aligns, centers, finds rest, slowing time to its proper speed in the light of eternity.

Love the Lord your God with all your might, and you become mighty in God's power.

The more we love God, the more we empty ourselves, and the more of His love we receive. The more of God's love we allow to infiltrate our lives, the stronger the air current under our wings to fly free in His love.

Mary Southerland is a speaker and writer with Girlfriends in God. When Mary's son was four, she received a call to come talk to her son's preschool teacher. Her adopted son had told all his classmates he was chosen but their parents were stuck with them.

Whether you were adopted or not, you are chosen by God. You aren't here by accident. Your family didn't get stuck with you; you were chosen by God to be born. You were lovingly fashioned and formed by a loving Creator.

Regardless of the details of your birth, you were not an accident – you were wanted and planned. God loves you special because you were created special; heavenly designed by your loving heavenly Father.

After thirty-plus moves and various travels, I encounter people who look or act similar to someone I've known in the past. No matter how close their appearance or personality, there are always differences, no one can replace friends I've left behind or those who have gone to be with the Lord. I'll always miss them.

Each of us are uniquely designed by God and because of that uniqueness, there is an ache, a longing, a crevice in our souls nothing and no person can satisfy – except God.

God has that same longing and desire to spend time with you. No one else takes your place in His heart.

God didn't create you to be like anyone else. You don't have to think, act, feel, or be anyone but you. You were placed on planet earth at a specific time for a specific purpose.

The love God gives is the love we all long for. He is The One who will cuddle next to our hearts when we cuddle up to Him. When our hearts are entwined with His, when we spend time with Him, we both find fulfillment. Through Christ's presence, we become the absolute best we were designed to be --perfectly loved reflecting perfect love.

God's love jettisons us into the heavenly jet stream. Oh but there is more, much more, to help us stay upright and in flight.

Gratitude changes everything. Through the lens of gratitude, what we have becomes clear, and what we don't have fades away. Gratitude focuses on blessings, not on lack. Eve had paradise yet I wonder if she had had been living in gratitude would she have even noticed and been tempted by the forbidden fruit?

Paul was beaten numerous times, stoned and left for dead, ship-wrecked, imprisoned, and suffered in terrible ways, yet he knew the secret of a thankful heart brought contentment. Living in thankfulness brings joy in spite of the realities of pain and hardship.

A heart of gratitude beats with joy.

A thankful heart beats with freedom to truly live.

A life with praise and thanksgiving is a life lived well for eternity.

Thanksgiving is more than a holiday, thanksgiving is a lifestyle. And the more we style our life on thankfulness, the more our eyes are open to see God's blessings, provision, faithfulness, and love.

Thanksgiving brings freedom to enjoy life and freedom to live above and beyond circumstances. We can always be thankful for the grace and mercy of Jesus Christ.

Thanksgiving replaces emotions with reality – the reality of a life that is eternal, that raises the soul above the painfulness and frailty of life.

If your life is good, be thankful.

If your life is hard and miserable, thank God that He will help you through and never leave you.

Paul, Peter, James, and others mentioned in the Bible didn't just know God, they longed to know the depths of God, the pull of the mighty depths of God that transcended fear from death, beatings, stoning, and living without earthly comfort. They lived beyond the difficulties of the day to stretch forward to the future.

Bible verses are one of the keys to living a joyful life and walking in freedom. When we know God's Word, we also are given the joy of abiding in Christ because we know how to live in Christ.

When Jesus was tempted by the devil, He quoted scripture. God's word is an offensive weapon. If we don't study, read, and memorize scripture, we might as well be twiddling toothpicks at the enemy instead of wielding powerful swords.

Jesus said if we keep His commandments, we will abide in His love, and His joy would be in us and that joy would be made full. (John 15:10-11) Fullness of joy is found in God's presence. Jesus is joy and lives in our hearts. One of the fruits of the Spirit is joy. Therefore, joy is always with us, and we can rejoice always because joy is in us and lives in us.

The more verses I read, study, and dissect, the more I find a common thread. Joy is found by spending time with God, obeying Him, thanking Him, reading His word, and praising Him (through word and song).

God's joy is the perfect picture of a perfect loving relationship. God is The One who won't ever misunderstand you and will know exactly what you mean even when words are jumbled, confused, a desperate whisper, or merely a groan.

Filtered by love, God hears and knows our inmost thoughts, emotions, and desires. Knowing we are loved and deeply cared for gives us the incredible blessing of talking with God through prayer.

We watched the movie *Gravity* with Sandra Bullock. Her character was in a life-threatening situation, and in her fear and anguish she comments that no one taught her how to pray. My heart broke. I longed to jump into the movie and tell her God was waiting to hear from her. I know it's only a movie, but I wonder how many people feel the same way?

How many people would love to pray, but don't feel they know how, have a right, or aren't cleaned up enough to pray to God?

Prayer is talking to God. To put it more plainly, prayer is talking to The One who made you, to The One who delights in you and loves you. You don't have to know Christian quotes or church phrases to pray.

You don't have to chant some mantra; you can talk to God freely and openly. Talk to Him like you would your best friend. God is waiting to hear from you. No concern is too small or too big. Nothing you say will shock or surprise Him. No difficulty or situation is beyond God's care.

Pray = communication.

Talk, cry, scream, whimper, or whisper. God is waiting to hear from you. If you aren't sure what to pray, read the Psalms and pray them to God. The Psalms deals with just about anything you might be experiencing.

I've used Psalm 23 to pray several times, and each time I come up with different prayers as I read. I'll share an example. The highlighted words are the actual Psalm, and then I add my thoughts.

Praying through Psalm 23

The Lord is my shepherd – He is mine and I am His!
I shall not want – His provision will come; His provision will always come.
He makes me lie down in green pastures – I'm sorry Father, when you have to make me rest. Help me to be completely willing to do Your will and rest in Your presence.
He leads me beside quiet waters – God, thank You for the beauty of your quiet waters, what amazing beautiful visuals You have given me to enjoy.
He restores my soul – Oh Thank You for Your restoration, soul-deep restoration!
He guides me in the paths of righteousness for His name's sake – Heavenly Father, thank You for Your guidance. Thank You for Your paths. Thank You that I am Yours and in You I am made righteous.
Even though I walk through the valley of the shadow of death, I fear no evil for you are with me. – Thank You that You are with me during the hard, scary, dark shadows. That even when death's shadows

fall, You are there.

Your rod and staff comfort me. – Lord, thank You for your correction, for Your staff of gentle guidance that keeps me close to You.

You prepare a table before me in the presence of my enemies – Thank You that even when I'm surrounded by enemies, Your banquet table is prepared and available for fellowship with You.

You have anointed my head with oil – Thank You for Your anointing which makes prosperous, takes away ashes, and fattens with good tidings.

My cup runs over – Lord, thank You for the saturation, overflowing love of Your presence.

Surely goodness and mercy will follow me all the days of my life – Thank You that even with my sinful past, the trials, hardships, and heartache, Your goodness and mercy are directly behind me, covering, healing, and restoring in Your grace and love.

And I will dwell in the house of the Lord forever. – Praise You for the honor and privilege of being Yours and having the promise of dwelling in Your presence now and forever. Oh thank You, Father!

The Bible is filled with honest situations and feelings that gives you words to help you know how to pray and communicate with God. There is power in God's word, so use His words to give you powerful words.

Jesus said His sheep hear His voice, and if you are a Jesus follower you can hear His voice.

Another thing I've done in prayer is to use the alphabet. I start with the letter "A" and think of a word that describes God, like Almighty. Then I go through each letter and think of a word that describes God. (A = Almighty, B = Beautiful, C = Compassionate, D = Deliverer...). As words come to mind, I use that to help me pray and focus on God.

Other times I've sang to God making my song a prayer. The Bible tells us to sing praises, and a song doesn't have to only come from a hymnbook. I've sung love songs to God because He's my ultimate love.

When we pray, when we talk to God, we aren't just talking to the air. We are entering the throne room of God.

I prayed on the phone with a precious friend. My prayers were good, fine, and acceptable. However, when my friend prayed, I was driven to my knees. My head bowed in adoration and worship. I'm still humbled by her prayer. My prayers were good, but her prayers led us into The Throne Room of our Mighty King.

I've been in The Throne Room, sat at God's feet, and marveled. Yet my heart breaks as I realize not every prayer is a Throne Room prayer. At times, in the familiar walk with God, I've forgotten His holiness.

Fervent prayers are power prayers. The Amplified version of James 5:16 reminds us, "The heartfelt and persistent prayer of a righteous man (believer) can accomplish much [when put into action and made effective by God—it is dynamic and can have tremendous power."

We are given God's power when we pray heartfelt, persistent prayer. Satan wants us to give up in prayer and give in to his lies that God doesn't care and won't listen. Don't let the enemy keep you from praying.

Pray beyond half-hearted prayers, pray BIG. When the enemy is hitting on all sides, fight back. Pray with passion. Pray deep.

Pray and remember no problem is too big for God and no problem is too small for His compassionate heart. Stand firm, keep praying, and keep believing. Prayers wing to heaven to help us fly through life.

Don't allow anything to block you. The enemy can't block your prayers, but disobedience can be a block prayers and blessings.

When God asks us to obey Him, He's offering the opportunity to live in freedom, not because He's taking away anything fun,

When God tells us not to lie, it's so we can be trustworthy and trust others because no one would lie.

When God tells us not to commit adultery, it's so our marriages are safe and everyone else's marriage would be safe.

When God tells us to stay sexually pure, it's so we can enter a marriage bed sexually pure. Guilt-free sex!

God's ways help us to fly in the freedom of His ways. His ways are really the **best** ways.

Obedience brings blessings. Every obedient action reaps a positive reaction. The circular truth again comes as we follow and obey God which results in blessings. And, God is the very best blesser!

I'm blessed to maintain several social sites. Although they take time, money, and effort, I love sharing God's joy and love. One day as I pondered whether or not to clutter my Facebook page with another post, I felt God's Spirit whisper in my soul, "Share the blessings, and I'll share the blessings with you."

Whether you are on the Internet or confined to your home, you too can share with others. Share what God reveals through your time with Him, or the things you've read, or the things you've experienced, or the things you've seen. We are blessed as we share the blessings of our time, skills, words, or prayers.

It is in giving, we receive. It is in sharing; we receive the blessing of sharing. In blessing, we are blessed. Bounce your blessings high, far, and wide because every blessing God gives us that we share with others, bounces blessings right back on us.

After our furniture was delivered in our Tennessee home, our Internet service provider came to install the service. The young man, Alan, was beyond kind and helpful. He did an extraordinary job. He answered all our questions and went above and beyond a typical install by making us feel welcome to the area. He was awesome! Later my sweet hubby talked to the main office and shared what a great job Alan had done for us. A few days later Alan dropped by to check in and see how things were working, and then he told us how he had been personally thanked by upper management. They had even played back my husband's phone call to share with him and the other workers.

Not only did they thank Alan, he received a raise and promotion. Woo hoooooooo! I tell ya, that made our day! We are thrilled for him and are still smiling.

God's word reminds us to be encouragers. When we encourage others, we receive back encouragement. Alan was blessed, and we were blessed to see him blessed.

Blessings are like flower seeds; they produce a beautiful harvest. So when you need a blessing, look for who can you bless. In blessing others, we encourage and receive back encouragement. And we all need encouragement.

Check out the definition of "encouragement" it is the act of giving courage, or confidence of success; incitement to action or to practice; incentive.

Encouragement gives courage to continue, confidence to continue, an incitement to act on courage, and an

incentive to continue.

While writing this book, I really needed encouragement to continue. We had moved to a new area and hadn't met any friends. Although my family is supportive, I needed someone to tell me I was on the right track.

When a friend sent me an email on how much she liked the book, I felt the wind gust back under my writing wings. Her encouragement gave me the boost of courage to continue.

Let's encourage, strengthen, and build up one another because this world is a tough place, and encouragement provides a soul-lift to keep flying.[61]

Encourage yourself with God's truth which will give you courage, confidence, and the eternal incentive to continue.

One area where encouragement is needed is in the waiting room of life. Waiting is hard, and our world is full of waiting. We wait in long lines, wait in traffic, wait for a phone call, wait for healing, wait for things to change, and wait for something positive. We wait and wait and wait.

Our family has been flying in life-circles during many waiting patterns. Many times we waited to discover where the Lord would lead us and where we would live. My sweet man was out of work twice for over a year. He had numerous interviews, but nothing opened for over a year (both times). Did I mention it was over a year?

I've prayed and waited for years for healing. I've prayed and waited for answers to problems that didn't seem to have a solution. My life has been stuck in many holding patterns, and there are times I've been so restless I thought I would burst out of my skin.

Can I just say waiting is hard? Difficult. Not fun. Taxing. And yet, **and yet**, God promises in Isaiah 40:31 that those who wait on the Lord will renew their strength, mount up with wings like eagles, run and not be weary, walk and not faint. [62]

I wonder how much of my waiting is because I'm so busy looking for the next step that I'm the one causing the wait? Even though I know God will move, lead, and guide, I am the one who has to trust.

Although I may see myself in a virtual waiting room, in fact my freedom doesn't hinge on what I'm waiting to happen. I am still free to write, do my chores, love my family and friends, and continue to do the things God has called me to do. The only one who has boxed me into a box is me.

In the wait, I have to choose to trust and believe, to rest in God's tender care. I have to look to Him, to run to The One who gives strength, and unfurl my wings to fly on the wings of love.

Now didn't that sound nice and churchy? Sorry about that. I grew up in the church, and the churchisms keep showing up. They come naturally, but let me put it another way.

On an airplane, you may be buckled into your seat, but you are still moving through the air. Buckled into God, our lives are always in motion.

Let's go back to Isaiah 40:31 to the Amplified version. Check this out, "Even youths grow weary and tired, and vigorous young men stumble badly, but those who wait for the Lord [who expect, look for, and hope in Him] will gain new strength and renew their power; they will lift up their wings [and rise up close to God] like eagles [rising toward the sun]; they will run and not become weary, they will walk and not grow tired." Isaiah 40:30-31 (AMP)

My sweet friend, Teena Goble, filled me in on some wonderful truths about the word "waiting."

"The word 'wait' is the word that

carries the idea of intertwining, much like what happens when we braid hair – the strands are woven together (intertwined) until they are no longer two or three separate strands, but one.

"The idea is that during the waiting season, God is using that time, and that process, to intertwine our will with His, so when He is finished, and the waiting is done, there are no longer TWO wills, but ONE — His.

"The word 'renew' is actually the word meaning 'exchange.' Exchange means we give up something in order to get something else. So the idea in the Hebrew is this: we give God our strength, and in exchange, He gives us His!

"Waiting is not a passive activity, but an active one. The process is so complete that it carries the idea of 'intersection.' It's the place where two roads meet, and in that intersection, it's impossible to tell which road is which. It works that same way in our heart – the intertwining process is so complete, that it's impossible to tell His will from ours – they have become so perfectly One." ~ Teena Goble[63]

I want that kind of intersection and intertwining! With God, that intersection and intertwining often happens in the wait.

There is an art to waiting, and waiting produces art. Sometimes the wait is a beautiful thing like a Rembrandt painting, and other times more like a Picasso. The choice of the outcome depends on us.

If I worry, whine, and complain about the wait, the waiting is difficult and messy. However, if I rest, trust, and praise God, the waiting is much easier. God's timing is perfect.[64] God knows the plan.[65] Trusting God leads to the blessings of trust.[66] Waiting on God gives us the power of God.[67] Resting, trusting, and praising God is an art mastered by remembering God's truth.

And the coolest thing God has shown me is, **if you live in the moment, you never have to wait.**

Oh, oh, oh, oh, I want to do that! I want to be trusting enough to embrace each moment. I make life harder than it has to be. Perhaps all I really need to do is be more like a child.

Small children can be fully in the moment of enjoying life, and Jesus says to come to Him as little children.

As I wrote this section on becoming like children, I started beating myself up because I didn't feel childlike. I've' turned into a stuffy adult. I couldn't think of a thing I really wanted to play. So, I ordered a coloring book with Bible verses and pages to color so I could get back in the child-like play mode. I still didn't feel very kid-ish, but I did enjoy the coloring and the verses.

Then I realized the little-girl Lisa was enjoying coloring and the big-woman Lisa was looking down her nose at little-Lisa. I had to tell the big-bully-Lisa to just bug off the little-Lisa and let little-Lisa enjoy her day! (Fist-bump self on realizing I can choose to play.)

For every action, there is a reaction. I can have a playful attitude and therefore find the playfulness in my attitude. Even in the hard things, even in the chaos of life, I can look for the bright spot and therefore see a bright spot. My brain can rest by resting and trusting God with the wide-eyed wonder of a child.

I may be considered a middle-aged woman, but I wish I could break out in a song and dance (and be good at it) in the middle of a store. Like on the videos where professional dancers show up in a shopping store or mall.

Or I'd like to accelerate in my mini-van past the guy in the sports car. Okay, I have done this once, and it felt so good. (He eventually won because I didn't want to go too fast, but my mini-van could have taken him!)

One day I stopped at a stop-light, and behind me a car with two men pulled up and waited. The guys didn't know in front of my vehicle was a Corvette. When the sports car revved the engine, the guys behind me stared in shock and amazement thinking the lady in the mini-van had some super-motor. That was fun, even if the fun lasted only a few minutes.

I digress...

I try so hard to "experience" joy that I often miss joy. I look so hard at outward experiences that I forget Jesus joy is inner, and His joy is eternal. And I NEED joy! Can anyone relate?

I need joy because joy is a soul-lifter, smile-lifter, face-lifting blessing. If I run back to Jesus (who is joy), I can find joy. If I point others to Jesus, they too can find joy. I will receive more joy because I will enjoy watching others plug into Jesus' joy, and the joy will multiply and grow for me *and* for those who run to His joy.

God blessed me with a great example. We placed a bird feeder and several other tasty options for our feathered friends. Finches, sparrows, and dove are our most common visitors. The finches at first puzzled me, and I thought they were terribly messy. While they eat, seeds fly right and left. Then I watched closer. The finches used their beaks to sweep side-to-side sending seeds scattering to the ground. The birds too big to fit on the edge of our feeder could now also eat because the tiny finches shared the bounty.

We can take the goodness of God and the joy of Jesus to a hungry world. As we share with others, our little wings catch the air current receiving a blessing boost as those who receive also are blessed.

Another important way to catch the heavenly jet stream is through thought control. I don't mean something weird, I mean taking our thoughts under the proper authority of Christ. That sounds kinda churchy so let me think of how better to write this...

Every day a zillion thoughts zing into my little brain, and if I don't get things under control, my brain will spin out of control. I have to choose what thoughts receive attention, and that is easier said than done.

Fortunately, we aren't left defenseless in the mind-control department. When we receive Christ as Lord and Savior of our lives, we are given the mind of Christ.[68] So how do we plug into this blessing?

Paul reminds us in Philippians 4:6-9 to fill our minds with the things that are good not the bad. It's like pushing out the bad air and breathing in the good.

Sometimes that's easy, but other times thoughts ambush from left field, attack in the middle of the night, or make us cringe in the light of day. Thoughts can come out of thin air, at the worst times, and send our minds whirling and tail-spinning into a negative mess.

Satan is like a ventriloquist; he throws his thoughts which sound like our thoughts to mess with our thoughts.

When bad thoughts taunt in the middle of the night or try to creep up during the day, pounce back with some quick questions.

"Does that thought bring me closer to God?"

"Does that thought honor God?"

If the answer is "no" to either of those questions, you are probably looking at an enemy attack. So attack back with God's truth. The devil flees when we stand on God's Word.

2 Corinthians 10:5 advises us to take captive every thought to make it obedient to Christ. So what do we do with those bad thoughts once we take them prisoner? Even when we lock them up, some of those thoughts can continue to torment from behind their jail bars.

For decades the enemy kept me silent and locked in a lie. During the times of past trauma, my throat would close, and I couldn't scream. The enemy planted a lie if I ever told anyone about what happened, he would again attack.

I lived in that terror for most of my life. When the time finally came to give voice to my fear and place it completely in God's hands, out came the lie. I voiced the lie in the midst of praying friends. And, God's truth set me free.

Anything the enemy wants you to keep hidden in the darkness needs to be taken before God's light because in Gods light is freedom.

Taking thoughts captive isn't just about shoving them behind mental bars; it is exploring God's truth and finding the reality of God's might, power, forgiveness, mercy, and grace. Total freedom comes from, and in, God's truth.

Knowing (truly knowing) God's word demolishes the lies and bad thoughts. The sword of the Spirit cuts off the enemy's lies. Pray, study, learn, and ask God to "send forth your light and your truth, let them guide me ..." (Psalm 43:3, NIV).

The enemy is always trying to mess with us, but we don't have to sit and stew in his mess. God's power is available to transform minds as we take those thoughts captive.

Take every thought captive, wrap it in God's truth and throw out the lies of the enemy. "We use our powerful God-tools for smashing warped philosophies, tearing down barriers erected against the truth of God, fitting every loose thought and emotion and impulse into the structure of life shaped by Christ" (2 Corinthians 10:5, MSG).

As for me, my voice is back. I can scream, and even better I can shout victory. Wield the sword of the Spirit and smash, demolish, and force those lies and bad thoughts to succumb to the power of our Most High God and Mighty Savior.

David prayed his words and the meditation of his heart would be pleasing to God.[69] Anything we think about or meditate on needs to be examined in the light of God's truth. If a thought isn't pleasing to God, it does not belong in your thoughts, throw it out!

Transformation is available through Jesus – mind, body, heart, and soul. You don't have to conform to the pattern of this world (how the world thinks, what they do, how they act), because if Christ is in you, the freedom of Christ is in you.

Take bad thoughts and evil visuals and expose them to God's light and the truth of His word. For in the power of The Light, thoughts are taken captive, evil is overcome, and you can fly free.[70]

If we don't expose thoughts and the past to God's light, we will be blackmailed. Satan, instigator and deceiver, sets us up to fall, then stands by with virtual camera in hand to capture images. He whispers, shouts, and screams our failures. And the problem comes when we believe Satan's lie that we deserve to endlessly suffer.

The enemy loves to torment us over the

times we willingly strayed off God's pathway and engaged in an activity we knew was wrong.

I've been there, done that. Not satisfied with God's best, I've traveled down the wrong roads. I ignored warning signs and headed over the cliff. I didn't just step my toes in the mud of sin, I went head first and wallowed in the pig-sty of sin.

Sin collisions always results in wreckage and out of the debris crawls regret, guilt, and condemnation. Satan is right there to rub our noses in the mess to blackmail us into ineffectiveness in Christ's Kingdom.

Christ came to set the captives free. Jesus Christ is not a part-time Savior. He is a full-time Savior. Through Jesus, the forgiveness of sins is available. God freed us from the power of darkness, and He brought us into the kingdom of His dear Son. As far as the east is from the west, He removed our sins from us. Christ set us free to live a free life. So if the Son sets you free, you are free.[71]

Remember in Christ...

You are a new creation.

You are not condemned.
You are an overcomer.
You are a conqueror.
You are seated in the heavenly realms.
You are God's workmanship.
You have been created for a purpose.
You are marked with the seal of the Holy Spirit.
You are led in a triumphal procession.
You are an heir and a child of God.

For in Christ all the fullness of the Deity lives in bodily form, and you have been given fullness in Christ, who is the head over every power and authority. Neither death nor life, neither angels nor demons, neither the present nor the future, nor any powers, neither height nor depth, nor anything else in all creation, will be able to separate you from the love of God that is in Christ Jesus our Lord. Rejoice in the Lord always. I'll say it again: Rejoice! [72]

Stay in God's air currents and fly in the freedom of Christ.

Flying on His Wings

Flying Forward

Have you ever watched old movie clips documenting those who first attempted flight? Men strapped huge wings to their arms and jumped from high locations in attempt to flap their way to the sky. Some fastened wings to bicycles or used contraptions resembling windmills. A few brave souls lashed rocket packs to their backs. The majority failed. Fortunately, people continued to try until the day came when man took flight.

Fear and failure have often kept me from flying forward. God reminded me of a ski trip I had as a child. That trip was paid for by a family friend. My clothes weren't adequate, and much of what I wore was borrowed. I didn't have lessons. I wasn't properly equipped or trained, but I had been given an opportunity to experience something amazing.

At the top of the mountain, I had tucked my ski poles and flew down the slopes. In my young mind I figured fluffy snow couldn't hurt, so I didn't waste energy going side-to-side. I flew down that mountain with full force, no fear, squealing with delight, total abandoned joy.

I want to live like that now. I want to fearlessly flying forward with God. Yet there are times I hesitate because I don't know what to do and I don't think I'm properly equipped or trained.

The Bible tells us we are called by God. We're called out of the darkness into His light.[73] Called into fellowship with God.[74] And called for His divine purpose.[75] The Greek definition of "called" is an invitation, an invitation to a feast, a divine invitation to embrace the salvation of God.

Y'all, isn't that amazing? Our calling is a divine invitation to feast with the King of Kings. When God calls us to do something, He is inviting us to feast with Him on a project. God's callings are a loving invitation which come with His divine power and strength to live fearless.

When little David killed the giant Goliath, little David didn't morph into a bigger giant, he relied on the giant strength of God.

When Gideon defeated the Midianites, it wasn't because of his power, but the power of God.

Moses didn't part the Red Sea under his own power, but because of God's power.

Samson killed a thousand men with the jawbone of a donkey.[76] That jawbone didn't give him the ability, God gave him the ability.

God's children are given God's power, strength, and ability. We don't have to wrestle with what we are called to do. We can rest knowing that what God calls us to do, He has equipped us to do in His power.

When wondering what God wants you to accomplish, remember Jesus said to love the Lord with all your heart, soul, mind, and strength. His last words to His disciples were to go into all the world and preach the good news. We have that same calling.

But does go mean going to headhunters and cannibals in some scary place? Probably not. There is so much more to the word "go" than just being sent overseas or to an undesirable location. The original Greek definition for go means to transfer, to continue on one's journey, to follow one, to lead or order one's life, go (one's) way.[77]

"Go" means as you are going on your way.

Go – Go inside your home, your neighborhood, state, country, in a foreign land, go wherever Christ leads you. Your mission field is with your family, co-workers, and friends. Going about your day as you visit with others, pray, or even while in a sick bed communing with God.

Tell – Tell others how Christ has changed your life. Tell them of the hope they also can find in Christ. Tell them of the grace and mercy through Jesus Christ. No matter who you are or what you have done, you can tell others about Jesus.

Make Disciples – Help others learn God's Word and His truth. Point them to God's love. A hurting world waits, and you are needed to help spread God's good news.

Tell others of God's grace and warn them of the consequences. Don't allow the enemy to silence the knowledge God has gifted you with to share with others.

You are never disqualified from sharing the beauty of God's love, grace and mercy and the new opportunities He brings. You are qualified to speak truth into the lives of others. Be honest about your struggles and failures (with Godly discretion) to point to the honest and unfailing, perfect love of God.

I've had friends with sinful pasts who feel they don't have the right to tell anyone else the correct way to live. Please, please, please don't allow the enemy to silence you. If you had a sinful past, you don't have to share gory details, but you can share the negatives and the pitfalls because of those sins.

The enemy would love for you to be quiet because that's how he continues to keep captives. When you share how God showed you the way out, you help someone else find the way out. Shine God's light on how He rescued you and others will be rescued.

Our past (even with our failures) are only stepping stones to step on the enemy to tell others how to step on and beat the enemy.

We are all given a mission field, and for years, mine was in the work environment, and then raising our son and teaching him about God. When I became ill, my mission field became the doctors, nurses, and patients I encountered. My current mission field is writing and perhaps tomorrow that task will change.

With God, there is a beautiful flowing of life. A call for a divine invitation to spend time with God and point others to God. As we share our verbal stories, we are provided fresh air for our souls.

When you share your God story and remember God's help, your soul is encouraged. The hope you have found in Christ, bolsters the hope for others. You resuscitate yourself, and you resuscitate others. We speak of the life we have in God, and The Life breathes life. Share your story and give soul-to-soul resuscitation.

To a world living in darkness, share the light.

To a world hurting and in pain, share the news of the One who heals, restores, and renews.

To a world desperately seeking love and fulfillment, share the love of God – the true source of unending joy and contentment.

When life's tragedies come, be there with a shoulder to lean on, a helping hand, prayers, encouragement, and love.

Spread the Good News, and love will multiply as we love with the love of Christ.

Peace will multiply as we share the peace of God. Blessings will multiply as we bless others. Life will multiply as life is freely given. Joy will multiply as we multiply the joy of the Lord.

Keep going! Run the race, and run to win your race. Keep your hand on the task at hand. Be diligent. Delight in God, and His will and He will give you the desires of your heart.

Whatever you do, do for God's glory, making your life a freewill offering to God. Keep up the good work, fight the good fight. Stay on fire for God by keeping the fire of God's word burning in your heart, soul, and mind.

God is faithful to complete what He starts. Keep going, don't give up, don't slack off, and don't let the enemy deter your walk in the Lord. Take ground by moving forward in your faith.

The Israelites were given the Promised Land, but they had to conquer those who already lived in the land. They were told "every place where you set your foot will be yours."[78] We live in enemy territory, but we are never defenseless.

Take the ground you have been given by God because nothing is impossible for

God, and there is no power, person, or situation bigger than God. Don't allow the enemy to steal your joy, kill your peace, or destroy how God wants to work in your life.

Keep going. Be brave and strong in the infinite strength supplied by God.

Keep your focus on Christ. Remember His promises, and remember He is always with you for now and through eternity.

Don't give up. Be the person God has called you to be. Keep praying. Be courageous for Christ. Love with Christ's love. Cling to God. Grow in Christ. Share the Good News with a world that so needs good news.

You have today. This day. You have this day to tell God you love Him. You have this day to tell someone you love them and share the good news of God's love.

You have this day to notice the flowers, trees, clouds, and sunshine.

You have this day to enjoy, to appreciate, to fully live the life you've been given.

Don't miss this day. Eject the baggage, trust The Pilot, fly through the battle, catch the heavenly air currents, and fly forward. Live in The Good News, share the Good News and fly, fly, fly!

Dedication and Thanks

Thank you to my amazing God and Savior, Jesus Christ. Thank You for Your grace, mercy, and love. Thank You that You beckon each of us to fly free on Your wings.

Soli Deo Gloria* – *To the glory of God alone.

About The Author

Lisa Buffaloe is a multi-published author, and speaker. She loves to encourage others that regardless of past or present situations, God's tender, unending love provides healing, restoration, renewal, and joy. When Lisa's not writing, she enjoys taking long walks with her husband and exploring God's beautiful nature.

Lisa is the winner of the Robin Award -- 2013 Idahope Christian Writers Writer of the Year, and her blog was listed as one of the top 100 blogs by Women's Bible Café.

Her novels placed as finalists in the 2010 and 2011 Women of Faith writing contest, the 2010 American Christian Fiction Writer's Genesis Contest, 2010 Great Expectations Contest, and received the Best of Conference Award for Adult Novel at the North Texas Christian Writers Conference in 2007.

The Forgotten Resting Place received First Place Finalist in the Global Media Summit 2020 Christian Literary awards.

Visit Lisa @ https://lisabuffaloe.com

Books by Lisa Buffaloe

(Updated July 2023)

Fiction

The Masterpiece Beneath
Nadia's Hope (Hope and Grace Series, Book 1)
Prodigal Nights (Hope and Grace Series, Book 2)
Writing Her Heart (Hope and Grace Series, Book 3)
The Discovery Chapter (Hope and Grace Series, Book 4)
Open Lens (Hope and Grace Series, Book 5)
The Fortune
Grace for the Char-Baked

Non-Fiction

Float by Faith
Heart and Soul Medication
Time with The Timeless One
The Forgotten Resting Place
Present in His Presence
We Were Meant for Paradise
One Lit Step: Devotions for your journey
The Unnamed Devotional
Flying on His Wings
Unfailing Treasures

No Wound Too Deep for The Deep Love of Christ

Living Joyfully Free Devotional, (Volume 1)

Living Joyfully Free Devotional (Volume 2)

Thank you for reading...

Flying on His Wings
Living Above Daily Struggles:
Taking Flight with God

Lisa Buffaloe

Notes and Bibliography

---

[1] *"Every good thing given and every perfect gift is from above, coming down from the Father of lights, with whom there is no variation or shifting shadow" (James 1:17, NASB).*

[2] *Jeremiah 29:11*

[3] *"The Spirit of the Lord is upon Me because He anointed Me to preach the gospel to the poor. He has sent Me to proclaim release to the captives, and recovery of sight to the blind, to set free those who are oppressed, to proclaim the favorable year of the Lord" (Luke 4:18-19, NASB). "So if the Son makes you free, you will be free indeed" (John 8:36, NASB).*

[4] *"The thief does not come except to steal, and to kill, and to destroy. I have come that they may have life, and that they may have it more abundantly" (John 10:10, NKJV).*

[5] *"And He did not do many miracles there because of their unbelief" (Matthew 13:58).*

[6] *Hebrews 11:6*

[7] *"And without faith it is impossible to please Him, for he who comes to God must believe that He is and that He is a rewarder of those who seek Him" (Hebrews 11:6, NASB).*

[8] *"[Most] blessed is the man who believes in, trusts in, and relies on the Lord, and whose hope and confidence the Lord is" (Jeremiah 17:7, (AMP).*

[9] *"Draw near to God and He will draw near to you..." (James 4:8, NASB).*

[10] *"Ask, and it will be given to you; seek, and you will find; knock, and it will be opened to you" (Matthew 7:7, NASB).*

[11] *John 16:33*

[12] *Exodus 3:14*

[13] *Hebrew definition of Forsake found in Strong's H5800 and Strong's H7503.*

[14] *John 21:20*

[15] *Matthew 8:3, 17:7, 20:3, Luke 19:5...).*

[16] *Luke 18:15-17*

[17] *"God demonstrates His own love toward us, in that while we were yet sinners, Christ died for us" (Romans 5:8, NASB).*

[18] *See Hebrews 11*

> [19] *Jesus said, "God is spirit, and those who worship Him must worship in spirit and truth" (John 4:24)*

[20] *"I no longer call you servants, because a servant does not know his master's business. Instead, I have called you friends, for everything that I learned from my Father I have made known to you" (John 15:15, NIV).*

[21] *Genesis 5:24*

[22] *"But God has chosen the foolish things of the world to shame the wise, and God has chosen the weak things of the world to shame the things which are strong, and the base things of the world and the despised God has chosen, the things that are not, so that He may nullify the things that are" (1 Corinthians 1:27-28, NASB).*

²³ *"And God is able to make all grace (every favor and earthly blessing) come to you in abundance, so that you may always and under all circumstances and whatever the need be self-sufficient [possessing enough to require no aid or support and furnished in abundance for every good work and charitable donation]" (2 Corinthians 9:8, AMP).*

²⁴ *"And God is able to make all grace abound toward you; that ye, always having all sufficiency in all things, may abound to every good work" (2 Corinthians 9:8, KJV).*

²⁵ *"Jesus has the power of God, by which he has given us everything we need to live and to serve God. We have these things because we know him. Jesus called us by his glory and goodness. Through these he gave us the very great and precious promises. With these gifts you can share in God's nature" (2 Peter 1:3-4a, NCV).*

²⁶ *"For the gifts and the calling of God are irrevocable" (Romans 11:29)*

²⁷ *Psalm 103:11-12, NKJV)*

²⁸ *"So if the Son makes you free, you will be free indeed" (John 8:36, NASB).*

²⁹ *"If anyone is in Christ, he is a new creature; the old things passed away; behold, new things have come" (2 Corinthians 5:17, NASB).*

³⁰ *"Choose for yourselves today whom you will serve ... but as for me and my house, we will serve the Lord" (Joshua 24:15, NASB).*

³¹ *"Go and report to John what you hear and*

see: the blind receive sight and the lame walk, the lepers are cleansed and the deaf hear, the dead are raised up, and the poor have the gospel preached to them" (Matthew 11:4-5, NASB).

[32] *"See to it that no one comes short of the grace of God; that no root of bitterness springing up causes trouble, and by it many be defiled" (Hebrews 12:15, NASB).*

[33] *John 5:6, NASB)*

[34] *"The sick man answered Him, 'Sir, I have no man to put me into the pool when the water is stirred up; but while I am coming, another steps down before me'" (John 5:7, NKJV).*

[35] *1 Corinthians 13:4-7*

[36] *"The Lord's lovingkindnesses indeed never cease, for His compassions never fail. They are new every morning; Great is Your faithfulness" (Lamentations 3:22-23, NASB).*

[37] *"... let us strip off and throw aside every encumbrance (unnecessary weight) and that sin which so readily (deftly and cleverly) clings to and entangles us, and let us run with patient endurance and steady and active persistence the appointed course of the race that is set before us" (Hebrews 12:1 AMP).*

[38] *2 Timothy 1:7*

[39] *Psalm 86:5, Isaiah 44:22, Isaiah 1:18, Lamentations 3:23, Ephesians 4:11-12, Psalm 147:3, Luke 1:37, Philippians 1:6, Matthew 28:20, Hebrews 13:5, Jeremiah 31:3*

[40] *"Have I not commanded you? Be strong and courageous! Do not tremble or be dismayed,*

for the Lord your God is with you wherever you go" (Joshua 1:9, NASB).

⁴¹ "The LORD himself goes before you and will be with you; He will never leave you nor forsake you. Do not be afraid; do not be discouraged" (Deuteronomy 31:8).

⁴² "Even to your old age and gray hairs I am he, I am he who will sustain you. I have made you and I will carry you; I will sustain you and I will rescue you" (Isaiah 46:4).

⁴³ "When you pass through the waters, I will be with you; and when you pass through the rivers, they will not sweep over you. When you walk through the fire, you will not be burned; the flames will not set you ablaze" (Isaiah 43:2)

⁴⁴ "The faithful love of the LORD never ends! His mercies never cease. Great is His faithfulness; His mercies begin afresh each morning" (Lamentations 3:22-23)

⁴⁵ "The LORD is my strength and my song; He has become my salvation. He is my God, and I will praise him, my father's God, and I will exalt Him" (Exodus 15:2).

"The LORD is my strength and my shield; my heart trusts in Him, and I am helped. My heart leaps for joy and I will give thanks to Him in song" (Psalm 28:7).

"Surely God is my salvation; I will trust and not be afraid. The LORD, the LORD, is my strength and my song; He has become my salvation" (Isaiah 12:2).

"The Sovereign LORD is my strength; He

makes my feet like the feet of a deer; He enables me to go on the heights" (Habakkuk 3:19).

[46] "Cast your cares on the LORD and He will sustain you; He will never let the righteous fall" (Psalm 55:22).

[47] "And my God will meet all your needs according to his glorious riches in Christ Jesus" (Philippians 4:19)

[48] Philippians 4:6-7, NLT

[49] "For God is not a God of confusion but of peace, as in all the churches of the saints" (1 Corinthians 14:33, NASB).

[50] *Wesley L. Duewel, Touch the World through Prayer, Michigan: Zondervan, 1986, p 138, 142

[51] Proverbs 4:20-24

[52] "The Lord is my rock, my protection, my Savior. My God is my rock. I can run to him for safety. He is my shield and my saving strength, my defender" (Psalm 18:2, NCV).

[53] http://www.blueletterbible.org/lang/lexicon/lexicon.cfm?Strongs=G4102&t=KJV

[54] 2 Kings 6:17, NIV

[55] "Enter His courts with thanksgiving, and into His courts with praise. Be thankful to Him, and bless His name" (Psalm 100:4, NKJV).

[56] Luke 2:36-38

[57] Matthew 14:23-27

[58] "And in the fourth watch of the night Jesus went unto them, walking on the sea (Matthew 14:25, KJ21).

new strength; they will mou[nt up with wings as] eagles, they will run and n[ot be weary, they will] walk and not become w[eary] NASB).

[68] 1 Corinthians 2:15-1[6]
[69] Psalm 19:14
[70] Psalm 19:14, 2 Corin[thians 10:5, Romans] 12:2
[71] Acts 13:38, Coloss[ians 2:13-14, Psalm] 103:12, Galatians 5:1, John 8[:36]
[72] Romans 8:1, 1 John [4:4, 2] Corinthians 5:17, Ephesians [2:4-5, 1 Corinthians] 3:11, 1:13, 3:6, Galatians 3:2[6-28, Ephesians] 2:14, Philippians 4:4, Coloss[ians 3:15, Romans] 8:38-39
[73] 1 Peter 2:9
[74] 1 Corinthians 1:9
[75] Philippians 2:13
[76] Judges 15:14-15
[77] Strongs G4198
[78] Deuteronomy 11:24

Flying on His Wings

*Living Above Daily Struggles:
Taking Flight with God*

Lisa Buffaloe

www.ingramcontent.com/pod-product-compliance
Lightning Source LLC
Chambersburg PA
CBHW061323040426
42444CB00011B/2753

9 780692 336724